UNDERGRADUATE RESEARCH IN MUSIC

D1707316

Undergraduate Research in Music: A Guide for Students supplies tools for scaffolding research skills, with examples of undergraduate research activities and case studies on projects in the various areas of music study. Undergraduate research has become a common degree requirement in some disciplines and is growing rapidly. Many undergraduate activities in music have components that could be combined into compelling undergraduate research projects, either in the required curriculum, as part of existing courses, or in capstone courses centered on undergraduate research.

The book begins with an overview chapter, followed by the seven chapters on research skills, including literature reviews, choosing topics, formulating questions, citing sources, disseminating results, and working with data and human subjects. A wide variety of musical subdisciplines follow in Chapters 9–18, with sample project ideas from each, as well as undergraduate research conference abstracts. The final chapter is an annotated guide to online resources that students can access and readily operate. Each chapter opens with inspiring quotations, and wraps up with applicable discussion questions.

Professors and students can use *Undergraduate Research in Music: A Guide for Students* as a text or a reference book in any course that has a significant opportunity for the creation of knowledge or art, within the discipline of music or in connecting music with other disciplines.

Gregory Young is Professor of Music at Montana State University and has held ongoing posts in conferences in undergraduate research and in curriculum development.

Jenny Olin Shanahan is Director of Undergraduate Research at Bridgewater State University, with leadership positions in the Council for Undergraduate Research.

Routledge Undergraduate Research Series

Undergraduate Research in Music (2017)

Undergraduate Research in Dance (2018)

Undergraduate Research in Photography (2018)

UNDERGRADUATE RESEARCH IN MUSIC

A Guide for Students

Gregory Young and Jenny Olin Shanahan

Routledge
Taylor & Francis Group

NEW YORK AND LONDON

First published 2018
by Routledge
711 Third Avenue, New York, NY 10017

and by Routledge
2 Park Square, Milton Park, Abingdon, Oxon OX14 4RN

Routledge is an imprint of the Taylor & Francis Group, an informa business

© 2018 Taylor & Francis

Library of Congress Cataloging-in-Publication Data
A catalog record for this book has been requested

ISBN: 978-0-415-78782-6 (hbk)
ISBN: 978-0-415-78783-3 (pbk)
ISBN: 978-1-315-22570-8 (ebk)

Typeset in Bembo
by HWA Text Data Management, London

CONTENTS

PREFACE

The Expansion of Undergraduate Research

Over the last 40 years in the United States, undergraduate research activity in colleges and universities has been increasing dramatically, led initially by science professors needing help in laboratories. Thanks to national organizations such as the Council on Undergraduate Research (CUR) and the National Conference on Undergraduate Research (NCUR), these activities have been spreading rapidly into all disciplines. In fact, even though CUR was started by chemists at primarily undergraduate institutions in 1978 as a way of collaborating with undergraduates in their research labs, the biggest division of CUR at the present time is Arts and Humanities. NCUR began in 1987 as a celebration of undergraduate research in any discipline, open to all colleges and universities, and currently registers about 3,500 student presenters and 500 faculty mentors annually. In 2011 the first British Conference on Undergraduate Research (BCUR) was held, and it continues annually with the recent addition of Posters in Parliament, modeled after Posters on the Hill in Washington, DC. The Australian Conference on Undergraduate Research (ACUR) started in 2012, and Australia also has Posters in Parliament now. The first World Congress for Undergraduate Researchers (WorldCUR) was held in Qatar in November 2016.

The primary reason that undergraduate research (UR) has spread throughout the world in every academic discipline is that it directly benefits students in a host of areas. Students who participate in UR are more likely to persist in college and graduate on schedule. They demonstrate significant gains in valuable skills such as critical thinking and analysis, oral and written communication, and logic and problem-solving. And student-researchers report increased self-confidence, excitement about their field of study, and clarity about future goals. The benefits of participating in UR have been so well established that the Association of American Colleges and Universities has identified it as a *high-impact practice*—one of the key aspects of a college education shown to make a significant positive difference in the lives of students (Brownell & Swaner, 2010; Kuh, 2008). Undergraduate research and other high-impact practices benefit students from every demographic group, major, and type of institution of higher education, though first-generation and underrepresented minority students show the greatest gains (Brownell & Swaner, 2010; Linn et al., 2015). Researchers concur that the advantages of participating in UR are most directly linked to the opportunities it offers for students to work closely with their professors in meaningful and profoundly interesting work.

Despite decades of evidence that UR is one of the most transformative pursuits a college education can provide, the majority of UR opportunities continue to be highly selective (often only for honors students) and limited to students in the laboratory sciences. They are not typically as available to students in disciplines such as music, where creative activity abounds, but "research" has not been the main focus, at least with undergraduates.

About this Book

We wrote this book to help faculty and students in the arts, and music in particular, become more accustomed to viewing what they do through the lens of "undergraduate research," especially when a more inclusive sense of scholarship and creative activity is included. The acronym URSCA, which refers to "undergraduate research, scholarship and creative activities," is seen by many as a more fitting way to talk about and recruit students to such opportunities. Creating opportunities for music students to participate in URSCA offers them access to a high-impact practice that may improve their cognitive and emotional development, acquisition of highly valued skills, and preparation for post-baccalaureate opportunities.

This book is organized in two sections. Chapters 1–8 cover some of the fundamentals of research methods, many of which are common to most disciplines and musical subject areas. They provide a foundation to help students get started in understanding research protocols and processes. Chapters 9–18 cover UR in musical fields that are taught in many collegiate music schools. Chapter 19 provides annotated online resources, but certainly not an exhaustive list. Each chapter begins with inspirational quotes, a chapter summary, and then an explanation of the substance of the chapter with examples and ideas for students to pursue. Many of the chapters have examples of abstracts submitted to conferences by undergraduate researchers across the United States. Many of the abstracts included in chapters 9–18 come from the published NCUR Abstract Archive (www.cur.org/conferences_and_events/student_events/ncur/archive) and are used by permission. Since they are just sample abstracts, citations are not fully referenced.

Music majors, from their first semester until they take their capstone course, can use this book as a tool to build awareness about conducting scholarly work in the broad field of music. In a senior "capstone" it can serve not only as the course textbook, but also as a more specific guide for the whole process of choosing a topic and seeing it through to completion. Completing successful undergraduate research projects in music and disseminating the results at conferences and in publications will promote this activity and serve as a model for other music students in the future.

Students: How to Use this Book

A brief glance at the table of contents reveals that this book does not necessarily have to be read in order, from the first chapter to the last. Instead, it is intended as a guide to be consulted throughout the different facets of student research projects. There is no one perfect way to progress through an undergraduate research experience in music, especially because there are so many different areas to explore. Music composition, for example, will be quite a different experience than a quantitative research study in music education. So with the guidance of your instructor, use the tools in the first half of the book as needed for your research/creativity, and read about a wide variety of student examples in the areas that interest you in the second half of the book. Be sure to glance through the online resources and delve more deeply into those sites and files that interest you. It might also be helpful to create your own set of online resources and have that handy for future reference.

Faculty: A Sample Music Capstone Course

MUSI 499R at the Montana State University School of Music is intended to give students in their final year the opportunity to synthesize various strands of their undergraduate training in music. At issue is an exploration of the ways in which musical problems can be solved. These problems include issues related to interpretation, analysis, composition, and understanding. In particular this course requires students to explore the relations among a variety of areas of research/creative activity in music, in pursuit of finding answers to musical questions. Further, in a culminating project students have to (a) choose a relevant and sufficiently limited topic and a specific question, issue, or problem posed with respect to this topic, and (b) use creative, analytical, musicological, and/or quantitative methods to shed light on this question, a process which might end in a performance, poster, essay, or a composition that puts this new understanding into practice. This book provided eight students with a capstone project—an opportunity for each to assist in the writing of a chapter. Seven of the students are pictured in the front of the book and one, Logan Henke, is pictured in Chapter 15.

Learning Outcomes

1   Students will understand the process that professors use to discover new knowledge in music and related fields.
2   Students will be able to connect the many subject areas they have studied in music throughout their undergraduate degree.
3   Students will learn proper procedure for preparing a new work for dissemination.

At Montana State University, when music major Anthony Gaglia was completing a composition and performance project just prior to graduation in 2016, he said, "This is the most fun I've had during my whole degree program." That love of learning, discovering, and creating is exactly what we want to get across in undergraduate research.

References

Brownell, J. E., & Swaner, L. E. (2010). *Five High-impact Practices: Research on Learning Outcomes, Completion, and Quality.* Washington, DC: Association of American Colleges and Universities.

Kuh, G. (2008). *High-impact Educational Practices: What They Are, Who Has Access to Them, and Why They Matter.* Washington, DC: Association of American Colleges and Universities.

Linn, M. C., Palmer, E., Baranger, A., Gerard, E., & Stone, E. (2015). Undergraduate research experiences: Impact and opportunities. *Science*, 347(6222), 627–633.

FOREWORD

This volume is the first in a series of books on undergraduate research. The pedagogy involved here represents one of the many high-impact practices in college teaching centered on active learning. The information contained herein should assist students and faculty in pursuing exciting projects linking student learning with the discovery of knowledge, and provide ideas about how to get started and a sampling of some of the projects already undertaken by others. It breaks new ground mainly because music professors and students in general have not all fully embraced the term undergraduate research, especially in certain areas, such as performance, composition, and music education. In parallel with the international increase in undergraduate research in all disciplines, more music schools are including this activity both in required courses and independent study experiences.

Gregory Young

ACKNOWLEDGMENTS

This book is dedicated to the 2016 Fall Semester senior capstone class at the Montana State University School of Music (MUSI 499R).

SENIOR CAPSTONE CLASS 2016 Front row from left: Hannah Lane, Miranda LeBrun, Rachel Wambeke, Anna Border. Back row: Gregory Young, Andrew Major, Susan McCartney, Daniel Chausse (photo by Leif Erickson)

These students each concentrated on a single chapter, and through individual research, class feedback, and professor mentoring, made valuable contributions to the completion of this book. Their research was presented at the 2017 MSU Student Research Conference.

Other undergraduate researchers who contributed to the book: Logan Henke worked independently on Chapter 15 and is pictured there. Other MSU students who made contributions are Jaimie Hensley, Mike Andrews, Anthony Gaglia, and Keeli Telleen.

Special thanks to Constance Ditzel at Taylor and Francis for being a sounding board for ideas from conception to completion, and to Rachel-Beth Gagnon from Bridgewater State University for help with copyediting.

We would also like to express gratitude to Beth Ambos and the staff at the Council on Undergraduate Research for hosting the NCUR abstract archive, and to Robert Yearout and Mila Lemaster at the UNC-Asheville for creating and populating it.

1

OVERVIEW

We are the music makers, and we are the dreamers of dreams.
Arthur O'Shaughnessy, "Ode" from *Music and Moonlight*

All of us ... can understand and feel the joy of being carried forward by the flow of music. Our love of music is bound up with its forward motion ... To stop the flow of music would be like the stopping of time itself, incredible and inconceivable.
Aaron Copland, "The Pleasures of Music"

Summary

This chapter describes the undergraduate research environment and where music fits into it, reframing some of the excellent creative work already being done in college and university music schools as faculty-mentored scholarship. Within that context, we explain the importance of undergraduate research, its desired learning outcomes, and how knowledge and art are created in the field of music. As readers of this book will discover, conducting research is certainly not limited to the sciences and related fields. Music students from their first year through final year can also participate in the thrill of discovering new knowledge and the engaging scholarly process otherwise known as undergraduate research. Undergraduate research is an interactive pedagogy that has been shown to be more engaging and successful than traditional classroom lecture-style learning.

Where Music Fits into the Undergraduate Research Movement

As learning in college becomes more active, and students desire greater input into their own education, undergraduate research, scholarship, and creative activities (URSCA) have become more significant. Since search engines like Google can help students find a plethora of content, and YouTube provides a great array of music and instruction at our fingertips, learning how to actually create knowledge, how to tap into our creativity, and how to advance the discipline of music, should take center stage, so to speak.

An undergraduate music degree, therefore, would not be complete without a substantial exploration into the discovery of knowledge in a variety of topics, from the way new music is created to historical revelations or rediscoveries in the field. Music majors should be engaged in innovative techniques, analyses, and practices throughout their degree programs. Although in-depth study is often undertaken in the latter part of an undergraduate program, ideally students should be exposed to the act of discovery and creation as often as possible throughout the music degree program. Early and frequent opportunities to think with creativity, imagination, and originality have been shown to influence further successful learning and study.

When students are asked about their vision for how they would like to learn, many say they want it to be exciting, applicable, social, and interactive. Doing group projects, working alongside professors, having input instead of passively listening, and helping to chart their own pathways, can all be components of undergraduate research in music.

When employers are asked what skills they want future employees to have, many list teamwork, creativity, problem-solving, critical thinking, as well as written and oral communication. All of these can be strengthened by a real academic experience in undergraduate research and creative activity.

There are many different terms for "research," including inquiry, creative activity, and creative scholarship. These terms are sometimes used interchangeably, though scholars in various disciplines often have preferences for the ways they describe their work. Many people involved in the Council on Undergraduate Research (CUR), especially in its Arts and Humanities division, use the acronym URSCA: undergraduate research, scholarship, and creative activity. Whether you prefer one term over another, or your university has a program that uses certain terms, the term itself does not matter as much as what is it indicates: scholarly work that is faculty-mentored, original, disciplinarily appropriate, and disseminated (Osborn & Karukstis, 2009). We generally avoid some of the specifically scientific terms such as *hypothesis* and *methodology* when composing a string quartet, for example, and could substitute terms such as *background research, motivic development*, and *compositional technique*. Students of music or any other field also benefit from the cross-pollination that occurs when considering how undergraduate research is practiced in disciplines that are quite different from their own, and when they explore the different terminology.

Opportunities for Original Research in Music

How can students do something original when professors, scholars, composers, theorists, and other music practitioners have already done so much research? One way is to take an interdisciplinary approach, viewing music from the perspective of another discipline. For example there has been little research published on the correlations between music and economics. Music and the brain offers topics that are ripe for discovery, especially with new advances in medical technology that allow even undergraduates the opportunity to view brain-wave activity while students are playing music. One example of this kind of interdisciplinarity began in 1991 when J.B. Bancroft, an architecture professor, approached me (Young) and said, "Have you heard the quote 'Architecture is frozen music'?" I said yes, and we started a small research project centered on terminology and sources of inspiration that were common to both disciplines. This led to us teaching an undergraduate research seminar for eight music majors and eight architecture majors. After helping us flesh out the important correlations between the two disciplines, the music majors were required to compose a piece of music based on a building, and the architecture majors had to design a building based on music they chose. Much of the student work was published in *Leonardo Music Journal*, an MIT journal, and the professors were invited to lecture in Italy, Tasmania, and Japan (Bancroft, Young & Sanderson, 1993). Thinking about other possibilities for interdisciplinary seminars, what subjects could be paired with music? Or another way of thinking about it is, are there any that could not be paired with music? Chapter 11 of this book is focused on interdisciplinarity.

Students do not have to follow such an interdisciplinary path, however. There are many standard activities in undergraduate music programs that students and professors have been engaged in for decades that have not been generally regarded as undergraduate research. An example would be analyzing a piece of music and then using it as a model to create a new composition. This practice goes back centuries, along with other similar activities, like arranging a piece of music for a different ensemble.

Almost every campus now has some sort of annual student-research symposium, and while they were formerly focused on scientific research, they are increasingly campus-wide events open to students of all majors. This change has been accompanied by a parallel movement toward greater involvement by students in independent research mentored by professors, as well as projects that assist in or complement faculty research. The symposia that feature student research presentations sometimes consist solely of posters, where music students have to try to fit their presentation into a science-based format. On other campuses, a variety of delivery modes are available, including recitals, oral presentations, performances, and videos. Whatever the format, with a little creativity, music students should be able to present in a way that allows them to communicate the results of their work effectively. Many universities and colleges are now stressing the importance of undergraduate research thoughout the campus, and students in most disciplines are doing research as a regular part of their education and presenting their findings publicly. Music majors likewise benefit from joining in. Campus-wide celebrations of undergraduate research are still dominated by the sciences and related fields. These symposia could be enhanced with greater contributions from the arts, including a variety of music projects. And directors of such events are often open to the idea of adding special venues for music-related projects and allowing different methods of delivery.

Can Undergraduate Research Benefit the Student *and* the Professor?

More and more, universities are emphasizing the integration of scholarship and teaching, linking student learning with the discovery of knowledge, and making active learning a hallmark experience of an undergraduate degree. One of the best ways to accomplish all of these is to have a professor carve out a small piece of his/her own larger research project, and assign it to a student. Examples abound in chemistry, where researchers can be much more productive in the laboratory with the help of undergraduate researchers, and the students learn the complex process of original research in their field. In the arts and humanities, and particularly in music, professors often view their research/ creativity as individual scholarly pursuits, and published articles and musical compositions are usually listed with only one author/composer. However, with a little creativity, win–win situations can be created that increase productivity for the professors and that provide first-hand experience on the front lines of the creation of art or original research for the students. The famous *Pastoral Symphony* (Symphony no. 3) by Ralph Vaughan-Williams contains some contributions by the then undergraduate student Neil Van Allen, who was a copyist. Several times, when he was unsure of the master's sketches, he asked him about the notes, and Vaughan Williams said, "Dear boy, by now you know my style, just put in what you think I would do." Another example occurred when I (Young) enrolled an undergraduate researcher, Samantha Tschida, to help survey students and faculty on the benefits of learning to perform from memory. The resulting article was published in a national journal (Young, 2003) and subsequently reprinted in two German journals (Young, 2004, 2006). This article would not have been written without this teacher–student collaboration, and the student was able to list the article and the activity on her resume.

Senior Capstone Course

University music curricula often have some kind of final course in the senior year, with titles such as senior recital, senior thesis, senior project, or capstone. Although not often referred to as undergraduate research, these most often are exactly that. Students preparing a senior recital are often required to write their own program notes; composition students need to be able to write some kind of artist statement explaining their process; music history and theory majors have a writing or analysis requirement; and the list goes on. Much of what we do in courses like this could be presented at campus, regional, national, or international conferences, because it represents the discovery of knowledge. See the sample capstone course and learning outcomes in the preface.

This particular course, whatever the format, is often cited as the most impactful single course in the curriculum for music majors. It is also viewed by many as the most challenging, both in terms of creative thinking and final product expectations.

How to Use this Text

Although intended as a text for senior project or senior capstone courses, this text can fulfill other functions. It should be an interesting read for all music majors, whatever their particular focus, and it can also be used as a reference for particular subject areas. The sample abstracts at the end of the topic chapters are just a beginning, there are many more online and in print. This text might also give students and faculty members ideas about other things they can do to increase the visibility and activity on their own campuses with respect to undergraduate research in music.

Conclusion

As the participation of music majors in undergraduate research increases, and the familiarity of that term as an umbrella term for many of the creative and scholarly activities we pursue, music degrees will become more engaging, more challenging, and more fun. Music will be viewed more as a scholarly activity by people in other disciplines and less as a service field when music is needed for a particular event.

Questions for Discussion

1 What is the difference between creativity in science and creativity in music?
2 How do the terms inquiry, creativity, scholarship, and research differ?
3 Why do employers prefer students who have done undergraduate research?
4 Do all professors do research, and how much do they need to do?

References

Bancroft, J., Young, G. & Sanderson, M. (1993). Musi-Tecture: Seeking useful correlations between music and architecture, *Leonardo Music Journal*, 3, 39–43.

Osborn, J. M. & Karukstis, K. K. (2009). The benefits of undergraduate research, scholarship, and creative activity. In M. Boyd and J. Wesemann (eds.), *Broadening Participation in Undergraduate Research: Fostering Excellence and Enhancing the Impact*, Washington, DC: Council on Undergraduate Research.

Young, G. (2003). Teaching students to perform from memory: A clarinetist's perspective. *NACWPI (National Association of College Wind and Percussion Instructors) Journal*, 51(1), 14–16.

Young, G. (2004). Auswendigspielen: Unterrichtsvorschlage eines Klarinettisten, *TIBIA: Magazin für Holzbläser*, 3, 185–186.

Young, G. (2006). Auswendigspielen: ein wichtig Bestandteil der musicalischen Entwicklung. *Rohrblatt: Magazin für Oboe, Klarinette*, 2, 76–77.

2

LITERATURE REVIEWS

The difference between literature and journalism is that journalism is unreadable,
and literature is not read.

Oscar Wilde, *The Artist as Critic*

Literature is an investment of genius which has dividends to all subsequent
times.

John Burroughs, *Indoor Studies*

Summary

A literature review is an organized, informed discussion of published works that
are significant to the subject of study. It conveys the relationship between the
present study and what has already been published in the field. By reviewing the
literature, scholars join important conversations in the discipline, with critical
understanding of what others have said, how the voices in the conversation
relate to one another, and where they might add insight.

Purpose and Format of a Literature Review

Conducting research on music and reporting on its results is a professional
way of joining a vibrant, ongoing conversation about the field. Contributing to
that interesting conversation entails understanding what others have said, how
the voices in the conversation relate to one another, and where further insight
might be added. To contribute meaningfully to the conversation scholars need
to study published material (the "literature") related to the topic. Much like
other reviews, a *literature review* is an analysis of that published material.

A literature review provides context for your research study by explaining what is already known and what needs further exploration. In doing so, it establishes your credibility as a researcher, demonstrating that your project or study did not emerge from "out of the blue," but from thoughtful consideration of what has been published already and how your work fits in to that framework. The literature review should accomplish three main objectives:

- briefly summarize the salient points of the most important publications on the topic of study;
- explain the relationships among those published works (e.g., how a major study changed the field, why some scholars came to differing conclusions on a key question, how the introduction of a new factor or variable in one study led to surprising results);
- identify gaps in the literature—the questions or issues that have not yet been examined.

That third objective, identifying gaps in the research literature, is critical to showing the need for your study. The literature review shows that you have read and analyzed important sources on the topic, and at least one significant question has not been addressed or has not been definitively answered. That is the gap your study seeks to fill.

Literature Review vs. Annotated Bibliography

The format or structure of a literature review is different from that of an annotated bibliography, which summarizes or describes one source after another in a few sentences each. If your professor assigns an annotated bibliography as well as a literature review for your research, you would complete the annotated bibliography first, as it represents your first pass through the relevant literature. Although annotated bibliographies usually include a brief evaluation of each source, each entry is its own individual item, listed in alphabetical order by the author's last name. The bibliography entries do not connect with each other except for the fact that they are on the same general topic. A literature review, however, is not a list. It is a narrative that could stand on its own as a coherent essay, with unified paragraphs and transitions between points. Your literature review allows you to "tell the story" of what scholars already understand about the topic and how they have informed your own study. Specific strategies for organizing your literature review are laid out later in this chapter.

Joining a Scholarly Conversation

Almost everyone has had the irritating experience of being interrupted from what had been an interesting conversation by someone who does not know what has already been said, but jumps in with opinions anyway. Sometimes the interrupter spouts unrelated ideas or rehashes a point from which the conversation has already moved on. The interrupter in such cases shows disrespect to the people who have already been engaged in the conversation as well as a lack of credibility. The group would probably dismiss the interrupter's ideas, even if they are potentially good ones, because they appear to be random and uninformed. For good reason, most of us have been socialized to join an ongoing conversation in a more respectful way: only after listening for a little while and gaining familiarity with the topic. A new person joining a conversation should ask or wait to hear what the group is talking about or allow someone already involved in the conversation to offer a recap.

That metaphor of joining an ongoing conversation is a useful way of thinking about a literature review. A "conversation" about the topic (or closely related to the topic) has been going on in the field, as represented in the published research literature. Reading the literature allows new scholars in the field to listen to what has been said and join the conversation as informed participants. Only by reading closely, or "listening" to, the previous participants' ideas can you contribute something original and interesting to the conversation, such as a new idea that has not been completely covered already or a question about someone else's point that adds an intriguing dimension to the topic. In other words, by conducting a review of the research literature you avoid "interrupting" a conversation with stale opinions or irrelevant questions; instead, you can knowledgably participate in a discussion of an interesting topic with a group of scholars who also deeply care about it.

Finding Appropriate Sources

Peer-Reviewed Sources

For most scholarly projects in music, the literature review will be based on *peer-reviewed sources*. Peer review is a process of quality control to ensure that articles and books accepted for publication are accurate and based on valid research methods. Academic journals and book publishers typically rely on rigorous peer-review processes before publishing someone's research. To be considered for publication, a researcher submits an article or chapter to an editor, who reaches out to experts specializing in the author's area of study to ask them to review it. Those experts are the researcher's "peers." Most peer reviews are *double-blind*, meaning that the researcher does not know who is reviewing the work, and reviewers do not know who authored it. Whether they are reviewing "blindly" or not, the reviewers are expected to evaluate the quality of the work impartially. They use their own expertise to determine whether the author conducted a valid and reliable research study, whether the findings or conclusions are sound, and to what degree the research makes an important contribution to the field of study. Peer reviewers usually can accept a work "as is" (perhaps with minor edits) or "with revision" (requiring the author to address particular questions or problems in the next draft). Otherwise, if the work does not meet the standards for research in the discipline, the reviewers reject it. Due to a rigorous process of review that determines whether a work is published or not, peer-reviewed journal articles and books are considered the best-quality scholarship. On the spectrum of reliable sources of information, one might think of peer-reviewed articles as opposite to "fake news" on social media. Any information simply made up by the author would be rejected by peer reviewers, who demand evidence of careful methods and accurate reporting. The professional reputations of a journal's or publisher's peer reviewers are as much on the line as those of the authors being published.

This book, for example, went through two peer-review processes. This book began, as most do, as a proposal submitted to a publisher. The proposal included an explanation of the need we saw for such a book, a proposed outline of chapters with brief descriptions of what would be included in each, and a sample chapter. The publisher forwarded the proposal to three experts in the field: music professors at different universities who mentor undergraduate research and have presented at conferences and/or published on the topic of undergraduate research in music—in other words, the reviewers were our peers. The peer reviewers each made recommendations about additional topics for us to include and other sources for us to consult, and they each recommended to the publisher that we proceed with writing the book. Once a full draft (a *manuscript*) was complete, it went through a different round of peer review, through which we received additional revision suggestions that made the final product considerably stronger.

If a professor or editor asks for a literature review of *peer-reviewed sources*, this is why: only high-quality research studies will inform the work. Researchers are unlikely to be led astray by false or unverified information when they stick to peer-reviewed journals and books. That said, it is sometimes acceptable to include non-peer-reviewed sources in a literature review, especially if the sources can be verified as reliable through other means (more about that later in this chapter) and/or if the topic of study has not received much attention yet from academic scholars. Consider, for example, a literature review on a contemporary musician or an emerging musical genre. Because the peer-review process takes time, academic articles and books are published many months after the manuscripts are first submitted. Experts in the music industry, however, may be able to publish informative articles in a popular press in a matter of days. An analysis published in *The New Yorker* is not a peer-reviewed scholarly piece, but it is reliable and therefore may be a valuable part of a literature review.

Library Databases

The best place to find peer-reviewed, scholarly articles is in online databases to which your college or university library subscribes. Starting with open-source repositories of scholarship such as Google Scholar is fine, but most academic journal articles are still found in subscription-only databases such as Academic Search Premier, EBSCOhost, JSTOR, and, for the purposes of music research, ProQuest's Music Periodicals Database, Gale's Fine Arts and Music Collection, and Grove Music Online, among others.

We recommend consulting with a reference librarian to learn about the relevant online databases for your topic area and how to access them. Many college/ university library websites offer online tutorials for using databases. If you prefer a tutorial in-person, a reference librarian may be able to walk you through the basic guidelines for the databases to which the library is subscribed. Knowing the specific parameters for searching each database (e.g., which truncation symbols and Boolean operators it recognizes) helps make searches more efficient and effective. Truncation symbols allow users to search for multiple, closely related words at one time. Some databases use # as a truncation symbol, while others use ★ (e.g., educa# for educate, education, educator, and educational; or wom★n for woman and women). Boolean operators are conjunctions (e.g., *and, or*) and other connecting words (e.g., *not*) that are used to include or exclude certain terms from a search. For example, a search for information about contemporary jazz musician Gregory Porter might use Boolean operators in this way: Gregory AND Porter AND musician NOT Willy (to exclude contemporary musician Willy Porter). Another option for that search in many databases is "Gregory Porter" indicating that only results with *Gregory* and *Porter* adjacent to one another will be found. A few databases, though, use single quotation marks for that purpose ('Gregory Porter') and still others do not use quotation marks at all to keep terms together. Until the unlikely day when all database builders will agree on a single system, consulting a reference librarian or a written guide to library databases is essential to finding the right information.

In order to identify relevant books and articles researchers use a variety of search terms. To yield comprehensive results, reference librarians sometimes recommend making a list of alternative terms and subjects related to your topic area and then conducting database searches using all of those terms. When researchers have trouble locating information, the problem is often that they have not hit upon the precise search terms used in the database. For example, someone researching "Canadian singer-songwriters" may find that using the terms "North American" and "lyricist" will yield additional results.

Experienced scholars know that the bibliographies of sources already found are excellent resources for identifying additional sources. By reading the titles of books or articles (and the names of journals in which they appear) on bibliographies, researchers can find a rich trove of additional texts to read. If the same source is referenced repeatedly, that is a good indication of its importance in the field. Similarly, when scholars find a particularly useful source, they search to discover what else the author has written and whether the journal has published any similar articles.

Analyzing Existing Research

In addition to being called "literature," the articles located through database searches are often referred to as *existing research* to differentiate those works from the original research you are conducting in your own study. Articles and books are also called *secondary sources* as a way of contrasting them from the *primary sources* that some studies utilize, such as musicians' diaries, letters, notebooks, and compositions. Secondary sources are articles and books that analyze (a) other texts (sheet music, lyrics, novels, poems, artwork, historical or legal documents, and other primary sources), (b) recordings (audio and/or video), (c) historical events and eras, (d) statistical or experimental data, or (e) people's lives, words, or actions.

To do the analysis required for a literature review, we recommend printing hard copies of articles and reading them with a pencil in hand, ready to underline sentences, circle key words, and take notes in the margins. When reading digital copies of articles or library copies of books, using a research journal (a spiral notebook is perfect) can substitute well for writing on a hard copy. Using a form of shorthand that at least you can understand later, you can make note of important points, key terms, and questions that arise as you read. That kind of critical reflection is the vital piece missing from inadequate literature reviews. Giving time and consideration to reflect on and position yourself in dialogue with the sources yields a much more nuanced and resonant study than the so-called "research sausage" that is created by throwing together a little from this article, a little from that book, etc. and trying to fit it all into the preformed casing of a "literature review."

Reading Reflectively

The following suggestions are a guide for reflective reading of articles in preparation for a literature review.

1   Read the abstract first, then the conclusion, before starting the body of the article. That strategy allows you to determine the relevance of the article to the study and, if it is indeed relevant, to boost your comprehension of its main ideas. After reading the abstract and the conclusion, skim the section headings and subheadings, and look at any figures or graphs. Then begin

reading with the end in mind. A clearer sense of the relative importance of each paragraph to the overall article becomes evident, allowing you to know which paragraphs can be skimmed and which need focused attention.

2   The "halo effect" is a cognitive bias that, in this situation, can lead a reader to assume that because an author's work is published in a peer-reviewed journal, the author must be "right," even though research is rarely definitive. As careful researchers read, they keep their minds open to various perspectives on the topic by alternately accepting the author's viewpoint and then raising questions about the research methods, limitations of the study, strength of the evidence, and the conclusions that are drawn. By following that model and raising questions and identifying the limitations as you read, you will help yourself in two ways: you will be able to draw more interesting and nuanced connections between sources in the literature review when you notice how each argument is constructed, and your analysis could lead to discovery of a "gap" in the research.

3   Approach reading as a multiple-draft process, not unlike the writing process. Scholars re-read some parts of each article, deepening their understanding with each return to the text. Academic writing, in particular, is densely constructed and written for experts in the field. It demands more than a single-shot reading to grasp its meaning and implications. Anyone new to reading and analyzing research literature is likely to feel lost in the complex sentence structures and specialized terminology. It is written that way not to confuse readers but to convey as efficiently as possible very sophisticated ideas to a highly educated audience. A metaphor we use with our students is that of a tightly packed suitcase: it took a great deal of planning and care for the author to use the space efficiently; as you "unpack" it you may need to move slowly, examining one item or point at a time, noting its significance before moving to the next.

4   Continually ask how each article or book chapter relates, specifically, to the topic area being explored. Could it help contextualize the problem? Does it show that your research question remains unanswered? Does it demonstrate how other scholars have attempted to address the question differently than your study will? In this way you can begin painless drafting of other parts of the research paper; for example, an article that corroborates the identified problem can be referenced in the introduction.

5   Learn the context for each source. Where does it appear (if an article)? What other kinds of articles does that journal publish? When was it written? Have there been more recent and/or more important publications on the matter? (The importance of an article can be determined in part by noting how often it is cited in other articles.) If it is an article that appears on a web site or in a periodical that is not peer-reviewed, how reliable/credible is the source? (See the "credibility check" at the end of this section.) If the source

is a book, what can be determined about the publisher? A university press indicates a peer-reviewed, academic source. Other publishers, such as the press that produced this book (Routledge), can be looked up easily in order to discover what other kinds of texts they publish.

6   Throughout this process, take thorough notes. When reading hard copies, we ditch the highlighter in favor of a pencil. Underlining points, circling key terms, and writing margin notes are more active tasks than highlighting. Interacting directly with the text on the page helps with retention of information, more thoughtful use of the material, and more sophisticated insights. When using digital sources or library books, take notes, with page and paragraph numbers, in a reading journal. That is helpful not only for efficiently referring back to sources, but also for keeping track of your thinking on a topic over time and how it evolves with each new piece of information. One strategy for fruitful notetaking is to write down what was most exciting, convincing, doubtful, and/or confusing about each article or book chapter, as well as what questions it raised. Engaging with the text and asking questions about it are essential aspects of joining the community of scholars in the field.

7   Keep meticulous records of bibliographic information (author, article title, journal title, name of the database, date of publication, date of access, and page numbers) in the research journal. Most of that information can be cut and pasted right into a draft bibliography. As too many of us know, unearthing that information later is frustrating work!

8   Learn the citation style expected for the literature review and use it in all notes and drafts. Scholars of music history and theory usually use Chicago or Turabian (a variation of Chicago) style. Music educators and music therapists use APA (American Psychological Association). Getting into the practice of citing the research sources in the correct form from the very beginning will save you time in reformatting later, as well as instill the citation rules in a hands-on, timely manner.

Checking the Credibility of Sources

Conduct a *credibility check* on the research sources that are not from peer-reviewed journals or book publishers. You should be able to answer "yes" to the following questions:

1   Is the article free of errors in spelling and grammar? Do the vocabulary and sentence structures seem appropriate for academic research purposes?
2   Is the author or sponsoring organization identified? Is the author qualified? Is the author affiliated with an accredited university, a nonprofit organization, or a government agency? (Qualifications and affiliations should be clearly identifiable.)

3　Is there documentation for the information provided, in citations and a bibliography?

4　Is the information verifiable in other sources?

5　If the article is from a website, can the purpose of the site be determined (e.g., nonprofit advocacy, business/marketing, objective information/reference, for-profit news, personal soapbox)? Is that purpose seemingly objective? (In other words, it should not be overtly trying to sway readers to a particular opinion or to purchase a product.)

6　Does it include a publication date or "last updated" date? Is it current?

7　If a website, does it contain its own substantive content, as opposed to mainly providing links to other sites?

8　Are links accurately described and still working?

Organizing the Content of a Literature Review

As stated at the beginning of this chapter, a literature review is an *organized* discussion of published works. It does not follow the order in which the researcher found or read each source; that would be a reading journal—not particularly helpful to anyone besides the researcher. And literature reviews are rarely organized in chronological order, beginning with the oldest publication and moving forward in time or beginning with the most recent and moving backward. It only makes sense to organize a literature review chronologically when showing the changing trends in the area of study is critical to your research. For example, a music education study examining how piano lessons for young children are typically taught in China today may need to examine whether Chinese piano lessons evolved from the teaching of string instruments (as the piano is relatively new in China) or from the changing approaches in the West to children's piano lessons. In such a case, a researcher could simply order the literature review from the oldest research to the most recent (or vice versa, as the case demands) and make clear that the sequential development is critical to one's understanding of the issue.

Most literature reviews are organized thematically, around a few main ideas. Strong transitions between each main idea show how one relates to another, such as how new methods evolved from previous ones or how scholars in different parts of the world or from different schools of thought pursued similar questions in markedly distinct ways. How does one (a) identify a few main ideas from many disparate sources, and (b) create transitions between them when they appear to be only loosely related? The strategy for accomplishing both of those complex tasks is to start grouping sources—and, usually, parts of different sources—at the time of reading. We recommend starting with big categories of the matters most often discussed in literature reviews: methods, findings, implications, and key characteristics of studies (anything in addition to the main methods, findings, and implications that stand out, such as a national study conducted in a very small country or the timing of data collection immediately after a major event that could reasonably be thought to influence results).

Organizing in a Table or Spreadsheet

As experienced researchers read and take notes on the literature, they also start to organize their sources, such as in a table or spreadsheet, which helps with subsequent tracking of patterns and relationships among the sources. Table 2.1 is an example of a table you might use to jot down salient elements of a few sources.

By jotting down key characteristics, methods, findings, and implications of each source, you can identify noteworthy contrasts as well as similarities. For example, the two or three sources that used *mixed methods* (a mixture of qualitative and quantitative methods, which is explained in Chapter 5) when most other published research on the topic has relied on quantitative data exclusively, could be discussed together in the literature review. Or, studies that came to vastly different conclusions could be juxtaposed for contrast.

Organizing in Narrative Form or Bullet Points

Some researchers prefer writing notes about each source in narrative form or in bullet points and then coding their notes for themes, patterns, and key differences. *Coding* in this instance refers to using different color highlights and/or different symbols (e.g., double underlining, asterisks) to mark patterns in a set of notes. For example, every mention of study subjects who are young children is highlighted yellow, while every mention of subjects who are adolescents is highlighted green. Or opposing findings are marked with left and right brackets (<, >).

The following questions may serve as prompts for the narrative or bulleted notes for each source:

- Is the significance of the author's work convincingly demonstrated?
- What are the author's theoretical approaches and/or research methods?
- What are strengths and/or limitations of the author's research methods?
- Was the study designed well?
- What are the main findings and their implications?
- Are the author's analysis and conclusions convincing?
- In what ways does the author's work contribute to the field of study?
- What are the article's or book's overall strengths and limitations?
- How does the work relate to your study?

TABLE 2.1 Organizing literature review notes

Authors	Publication date	Key characteristics of the study	Method and/or measures	Findings	Implications and my evaluation

Moving from Notes to Draft

Whether in a table, highlighted jottings, annotated bullet points, or other format, your organized notes about the research literature will help lead to the identification of patterns or other categories of information, known as *themes*. Each of the themes that emerge can become a paragraph or series of paragraphs of the literature review. Organizing the discussion of the research literature by themes highlights connections among the works under review. Such organization also demonstrates to the audience that you have conducted reflective and thoughtful research that has led to intriguing insights.

For it is your organized evaluation and analysis of the various sources' methods, evidence, findings, limitations, etc. that will give the literature review shape as an interesting argument. You will bring the research literature to life, so to speak, by moving well beyond summarizing key studies and even beyond noting some patterns. By organizing the literature review and choosing which sources to group with which and explaining how sources evolve from and/or dispute one another, you can make a unique set of claims about the literature on your topic of inquiry.

A well-organized, analytical literature review sets the stage for what comes next: the research questions to be examined in your study. For that reason, the conclusion of the literature review is the most important part. The last paragraph establishes where the existing literature leaves off and the present research proceeds. It demonstrates the need for the present study and what it will contribute to current knowledge.

Questions for Discussion

1   Is a literature review important for all projects?
2   How do literature reviews vary by subject area?
3   How do you know if your literature review is sufficient?

3
CHOOSING TOPICS AND FORMULATING APPROPRIATE RESEARCH QUESTIONS

The practical man is the adventurer, the investigator, the believer in research, the asker of questions, the man who refuses to believe that perfection has been attained.... There is no thrill or joy in merely doing that which any one can do ... It is always safe to assume, not that the old way is wrong, but that there may be a better way.

Henry Harrower, *Think*

Summary

This chapter discusses the importance of formulating a research question that is unanswered, yet answerable, and the processes that could be used to address it. It is essential that the development of research questions and refining of a research topic occur after, and are informed by, a thorough literature review. Many times, undergraduate students' initial suggestions for research topics are much too broad in scope, and a literature review would quickly reveal this. An example would be the topic "best ways to teach middle-school music lessons." Conversely, it is problematic when students' ideas are too narrow in scope, such as: "Have most high-school band students had private lessons before?" If a question can be answered with a simple "yes" or "no" answer, it isn't appropriate for a research study. Occasionally, when students are formulating a research question, they communicate with a professor outside of the music discipline, who can offer a different perspective. Such co-mentorship broadens the base of expertise from which students can draw.

Brainstorming Topic Areas

In order to generate ideas for a topic of research that is focused, timely, and of keen interest in your field of study, brainstorm responses to the following questions:

1 What are some interesting topics of conversation among you and your friends that relate to being a musician, studying music for your major, and/ or pursuing a career in music?
2 On the other hand, what topics rarely discussed by your friends seem significant to you?
3 Are there any trends in the technology or practice of music that you have embraced or resisted?
4 Do you disagree with the "conventional wisdom" on a particular philosophy, practice, or stance in the field of music?
5 Have you recently come to value something in your studies that had not previously seemed important to you?
6 Where are many people in your field of study going wrong (in your humble opinion)?
7 What are you most interested in learning about or contributing to in your intended career?

Refining the Topic

Starting with a broad topic area when embarking on a research study is common and perfectly acceptable. You might begin with a general interest in an area of study, such as how innovations in robotics are changing music composition, why Beethoven stands out among his contemporary composers, or what makes middle-school music lessons most effective. You might even think that if you are taking on a long-term research project of a whole semester or more you will need a large topic to sustain the work all that time. Ironically, however, the opposite is usually true. A significant, long-term research study requires a specific, focused question. Getting the scope of that question right is the most valuable task to accomplish early in the research process.

The preliminary research and brainstorming you put into refining the topic is well worthwhile because, as we and our colleagues have seen repeatedly with our students' research (not to mention our own scholarly work), the scope of the question can make or break the project. Imagine trying to carry out a comprehensive study of how robotics are changing music composition. Within that broad topic area there are dozens of possible approaches. For example, would it be a study about the algorithms written for computer compositions? Is it a philosophical exploration of what makes music "human" when technology is utilized more and more often? And what is even meant by "robotic compositions"? Simple melodies mimicking the style of human composers? Mash-up or hybrid compositions by humans assisted by computer programs? Or completely "original" creations of artificial intelligence?

As would be the case for that robotic compositions example, topics that are too broad can cause frustration and lead to wasted time. If it turned out you were most interested in the philosophical debate about the authorship of music that is composed by a robot which was programmed by a human, you would likely be reading some theories about the role of technology in human creativity, rather than, say, studying the algorithms and writing code for your own jazz bot. Each of those approaches is significant and time-intensive in its own right. Skipping around multiple areas of a broad topic area results in a shallow and/ or chaotic exploration. The clearer your focus, the more efficiently you can use your time and resources to conduct an in-depth, well-informed study.

Using the Literature Review and Plenty of Time to Focus the Question

Your review of the literature, as well as conversations with your professors, peers, and perhaps external experts, will allow you to understand what others have said about the topic and, in the process, help focus and refine your area of inquiry. By posing questions, analyzing the problem, and imagining various solutions, you will come to a deeper, more thorough comprehension of what is at issue and how to address it most effectively. This period of refining the topic into a strong, focused research question will be most valuable and satisfying if you give yourself adequate time and reflective space, as well as permission to scrap some ideas and begin again.

Very few scholars arrive at a perfectly refined research question through a singular epiphany. Most of us, most of the time, have to wallow around in half-formed ideas, mistaken directions, and—most frustrating of all—pursuits that have to be abandoned after days or even weeks of seemingly wasted work. Rather than fearing or trying to avoid "wasted" time—and, as a result, ending up with a simplistic or otherwise ineffectual project—try to see this time as an essential and valuable part of the process of creatively and comprehensively addressing a complex issue. If you are truly confronting a focused, significant, and problematic question—one with no single, agreed-upon solution—you will need to invest in a few good stumbling-around periods.

Guiding Questions for Refining a Topic

Taking time for focusing and refining your question does not need to be wasted time; in fact, it can be time incalculably well spent, particularly if you are engaging some critical, foundational questions:

1 Why is the topic or question important? To whom is it important? Are particular groups of people affected more than others?

2 What gives the topic tension? What would draw readers to learning more about it?

3 Read at least five current (i.e., usually published in the last five years) research articles about your topic and imagine yourself as a participant in a dialogue with the authors of the articles. What are the questions you would ask them? What seems to be missing or undervalued?

4 What are the sources of the problem or question? Complex questions usually have complex webs of potential causes. Can you identify some of the strands of that web? Do you know professors or outside experts who can help?

5 What is the history or broader context of the topic? To get a handle on the context of your topic area, use reliable, general resources available through many college and university library websites, such as *Oxford Music Online* or the *Continuum Encyclopedia of Popular Music of the World*, which includes large sections on social and cultural dimensions of music history as well as global music industries.

6 What other subject areas is your topic part of or related to? Might those other areas provide additional perspectives and/or interdisciplinary possibilities for research?

7 Why do you care about the topic area? What is its connection to your personal experiences or interests? In what ways does the interest extend beyond yourself, to other scholars and professionals in the field?

8 Who is the principal audience you want to reach with your research results? What do you want the audience to do as a result of your research: adjust their thinking about the issue? Change some aspect of their practices/work/ activities? Provide support (e.g., funding, advocacy)? Experience something new?

Freewriting

Write down your responses to these questions and other ideas that come to you. Writing is the best way to reach clarity and insight about the issue you are exploring. Instead of trying to brainstorm only in your mind, we strongly recommend putting pen to paper or fingers to keyboard and *freewriting* your ideas for at least ten minutes at a time. Do not suppress any ideas even if they seem flawed, and do not do any editing for correctness. The kinesthetic act of writing (moving a pen across paper or typing on a keyboard), along with the mental "unblocking" of ideas, lead to insights that simply do not arrive if you stare at a blank screen or piece of paper. Freewriting is a wonderfully simple and highly effective means of getting past "writer's block" or just getting off the "starting block" of any writing task.

Professor Peter Elbow, who has defined the drafting and revision process for college students for decades, explains the process of freewriting in his classic 1973 text *Writing Without Teachers*:

> The idea is simply to write for ten minutes (later on, perhaps fifteen or twenty). Don't stop for anything. Go quickly without rushing. Never stop to look back, to cross something out ... to wonder what word or thought to use, or to think about what you are doing. If you can't think of a word or a spelling, just use a squiggle or else write, "I can't think of it." Just put down something.
>
> (Elbow, 1973, p. 1)

Freewriting allows you to get past your own internal critic and tap into subconscious, creative ideas that are difficult to access any other way (Boice, 1993). Such active brainstorming will produce a lot of material—plenty to throw out eventually, but also some rich ore that you may not have uncovered without journaling. The added bonus: you have notes for writing a first draft later. Even decades into our academic careers we use this freewriting strategy at the outset of new projects and when writer's block hits. Something almost magical often occurs at about the 10-minute mark of freewriting: a breakthrough of an exciting idea, more clarity about a muddled topic, or the concept for a new and better direction.

Topic Areas in Music

Undergraduate research in Music often takes the form of one of the following broad areas. (Many more possible topics can be found in Chapters 9–18.)

1. Music History

Examples: social implications of Chopin's ballades; discoveries of European Jewish composers' works created during the Holocaust; Isaac Albeniz and the Andalusian musical tradition.

2. Ethnomusicology

Examples: how Asian folk music influenced twenty-first-century composers; the popularity of the Gamelan in university music schools.

3. Original Composition

Examples: orchestration of large-scale music composition; composing piano music for ancient works of Chinese poetry.

4. Music Education

Examples: how emerging technologies are influencing students' aural perceptions; how outreach programs can benefit middle-school students as well as their college-student mentors.

5. Music Performance

Examples: a performance of an out-of-print work, accompanied by program notes researched and written by the undergraduate; a premiere of a composition by a local composer.

6. Music Therapy

Examples: clinical applications of percussion techniques; effects of music listening on Alzheimer's patients.

7. Music Technology

Examples: experiments in musical expression using a MIDI wind controller; manipulation of recorded bird sounds for use in film scoring.

As each of the examples indicate, undergraduate research in music invites you to explore something different from what has been done in the past. It absolutely should be something uncertain, risky, or challenging—something that takes you from familiar practices and assumptions to new and surprising ones. Of course trying something uncertain, risky, or challenging can be daunting and uncomfortable, but it is essential to an interesting and purposeful study.

Designing a Research Study or Project

Investing time in focusing and refining your topic of inquiry undoubtedly helped you revise your research question. You are ready to develop and carry out your research plan, including creating a timeframe and figuring out logistics.

Will you be working with human participants in your research? Will you be distributing a survey, conducting interviews or focus-group discussions, recruiting volunteers, or asking people to try a particular intervention? If your answer is yes to any of those questions, or if you are otherwise interacting with people online or in-person (other than with your professors or librarians) for any part of your research, you need approval or exemption from your university's institutional review board (IRB) (see Chapter 4 about research involving human participants). In the meantime, for the sake of planning your research, be sure to build in time to write an IRB application, have it reviewed, and to make any amendments to your research that the IRB could require.

Freewrite/brainstorm responses to the following questions to help you design your plan:

1   If people will be involved in your research (survey-takers, interviewees, etc.), what is your goal for the "sample size" (number of people to recruit)? What are their key characteristics (e.g., college students majoring in STEM, adults who learned to play an instrument after age 20, fans of a particular music genre)? How will you recruit the participants you need? How will you reduce bias in your sample?

2   How will your study be different from what has been done by previous scholars (especially if it is similar to research in the literature)?

3   How does your study reflect "best practices" in the field, promote diversity and inclusion, and engage with timely and significant matters?

4   Is your research question large enough that it should be broken into two or three parts? "Unpacking" a research question into two or more stages or facets of the research can help organize your timeline as well as your eventual research paper. For example, assessing the effectiveness of a community music outreach program could involve the following facets: a) surveys of the people on the receiving end; b) interviews with the organizers; c) focus groups with the people providing the service. Each could be written up separately, followed by a summation paper bringing all three together.

Organizing a Timeline

Such brainstorming and figuring out the parts of your research design can lead to the creation of an organized timeline. The example in Table 3.1 is set up for a two-semester thesis. Of course yours should account for the time you have for your particular study. Keep adding to it as you realize additional facets of the project.

Purpose Statements

In many forms of academic research, scholars state the purpose of their study or project in one or two sentences. Stating directly and succinctly the purpose of your study clarifies it for yourself at the outset, as well as for your future readers. After the purpose statement, state the research question or questions that will be guiding your study.

Example 1: The purpose of this study is to …
Guiding the design of this study are the following questions:

Example 2: This research project examines …
The following questions determined the focus of the research:

TABLE 3.1 Timeline template

What do I need to do in the next week?	2–3 weeks from now (dates:)	4–6 weeks from now (dates:)	2–3 months from now (dates:)	3–6 months from now (dates:)	6–8 months from now (dates:)

Briefly articulating your study's purpose and identifying a manageable number of research questions can keep you on task. Write down your purpose and most critical research questions and post them at your work space. Just about any research study can easily mushroom into an overly ambitious project, particularly if you are doing a good job of reading related literature and considering multiple perspectives. Having the parameters of your study posted right in front of you may help you resist the temptation to totalize—to take on more than you can reasonably investigate, at least for now, in the attempt to be comprehensive.

Additional Mentors

Especially in music, there are many specialty areas and subdisciplines, including all the common band and orchestra instruments, in which different professors have expertise. Therefore students can usually find certain professors who have an interest in the topic they are planning to research. Even if professors with the right expertise are not your instructors, one of them might be interested enough in the topic to be an additional mentor, or might have a research project already in progress that could benefit from the assistance of an undergraduate researcher.

Interdisciplinary student projects particularly lend themselves to more than one faculty mentor. *Interdisciplinary* describes work that emerges from more than one academic discipline's knowledge base, research methods, ways of knowing (or *epistemologies*), and scholarly values. The two or more disciplines shape the work together, resulting in an approach and findings that could not be achieved through a single disciplinary perspective. Consider, for example, the interdisciplinary fields of music education and music therapy; for research in those areas, students may need expert guidance not only from music professors but also from scholars who know about educational principles or psychotherapy, respectively. One of the examples of music therapy research topics provided above, *effects of music listening on Alzheimer's patients*, came from a student project that was co-mentored by faculty members in music and in psychology. The psychology professor was a neuropsychologist who worked with patients with degenerative neurological disorders, including Alzheimer's disease. Her expertise, as well as her access to research participants, were essential to the study.

Will Success Be Measurable?

The ways to measure success will vary greatly depending on the particular topic, but some components of research success include whether or not the project allows you to make an *original discovery* of something you and your mentor did not fully expect to find; whether some *new knowledge* is created, even if that knowledge is different from the anticipated results; and if the findings indicate an *advancement of the discipline*, even in a small way. Successful dissemination of results, covered in depth in Chapter 8 of this book, is also a measure of success. Dissemination could be through a presentation or publication, or both.

Questions for Discussion

1 How do I know when I have a good research question?
2 When do I have to be sure of my topic and my research question?
3 What should be on the checklist for choosing a topic/question?

References

Boice, R. (1993). Writing blocks and tacit knowledge. *The Journal of Higher Education*, 64(1), 19–54.
Elbow, P. (1973). *Writing Without Teachers*. New York: Oxford University Press.

4
WORKING WITH HUMAN SUBJECTS

Genetically speaking, humans are terrible research subjects. We're genetically promiscuous—we mate with anyone we choose—and we don't take kindly to scientists telling us who we should reproduce with. Plus, unlike plans and mice, it takes decades to produce enough offspring to give scientists much meaningful data.

Rebecca Skloot, *The Immortal Life of Henrietta Lacks*

Research is formalized curiosity. It is poking and prying with a purpose.

Zora Neale Hurston, *Dust Tracks on a Road*

Summary

The focus of this chapter is human subjects research. We define and discuss the role of the university institutional review board (IRB) in reviewing, approving, and monitoring research involving human subjects, or human participants, in order to ensure that all research is conducted in accordance with federal, institutional, and ethical guidelines. We provide an overview of the Collaborative Institutional Training Initiative (CITI training), including information for students about what to expect and a rationale for participating in the training. A brief synopsis of Rebecca Skloot's book *The Immortal Life of Henrietta Lacks* is included as a means of illustrating the far-reaching effects of unethical research methods, even when the researcher is well-intentioned. The chapter concludes with a brief overview of types of music projects requiring IRB approval and CITI training.

Human Subjects Research

Any type of research that involves people—people who take a survey, people who are interviewed, people who participate in an experiment or study, etc.— is *human subjects research* or *human participants research*. A particular group of humans—what they think, how they change, what they do—is a subject of the research. Even if a very small part of the research includes people, even if the people are minimally consulted, and/or even if only one or two people are affected, the rules of human subjects research apply.

Human Subjects or Human Participants?

The traditional term *human subjects* is still used in most training programs and U.S. federal guidelines, including those governing research conducted by the Department of Health and Human Services. Since the 1980s, though, largely due to the work of those engaged in research into the AIDS epidemic, the term *human participants* has often been used to refer to the people involved in a research study of any kind (Bayer, 1995). When AIDS was first identified, those who had contracted the disease, especially gay men and people who had used intravenous drugs, were acutely vulnerable to social stigma as well as incarceration. Homosexuality was considered a crime in over half of the states in the U.S., was a disqualifier for teaching jobs and military service, and was often used as grounds for taking away parental rights. AIDS researchers needed to take thorough care not only to protect identifying information of patients, but also to ask questions with keen sensitivity and without apparent judgment regarding patients' sexuality or drug use.

> In a remarkable and quite unusual process, all the more striking since it occurred during the conservative Reagan years, representatives of gay organizations entered into a complex set of negotiations over the nature of the confidentiality protections that were to be afforded to AIDS research subjects.
>
> (Bayer, 1995, para. 12)

Together, leaders of gay rights organizations and medical researchers established standards for informed consent that effectively changed the role of AIDS patients in the research process from *subjects* to *participants*.

A *participant* is an active and willing member who is voluntarily contributing to the work, while the term *subject* implies passivity—the person on whom research is conducted. As this chapter's first epigraph quotation from Rebecca Skloot implies, research involving humans is vastly different from research conducted on more easily observable and controllable subjects such as plants and even mice. The main difference lies in humans' ability and right to choose what they do and what is done to them. Humans must be fully informed about research in which they participate, so they can either consent or not to the study.

Informed Consent

Informed consent is fundamental to conducting research with humans that is legal and ethical. As bioethicist Jessica De Bord (2014) explained, *informed consent* traditionally refers to the process by which a competent adult agrees to, or refuses, a medical procedure, based on thorough understanding of the reasons it is being recommended and its potential benefits and risks. Informed consent originates in the legal and ethical rights of adults to determine what happens to their own bodies (De Bord, 2014). Informed consent laws now extend far beyond medical procedures to all forms of research or intervention involving people. People can benefit from and be harmed by a much broader realm of research than that involving medical procedures. Imagine for a moment a psychological study that could trigger post traumatic stress disorder (PTSD) in some subjects/participants. Because myriad forms of research involving human beings have the potential for harm, no matter how seemingly minor, ethics and federal laws require that people participating in surveys, questionnaires, research observations, focus groups, interviews, oral histories, and any other form of research give informed consent to participate.

The Immortal Life of Henrietta Lacks

The 2010 book by Rebecca Skloot, *The Immortal Life of Henrietta Lacks,* was researched for over a decade to bring to light the far-reaching consequences and injustices of unethical research practices. It is about

> a poor black tobacco farmer whose cells—taken without her knowledge in 1951—became one of the most important tools in medicine, vital for developing the polio vaccine, cloning, gene mapping, in vitro fertilization, and more. Henrietta's cells have been bought and sold by the billions, yet she remains virtually unknown, and her family can't afford health insurance.
>
> (Skloot, 2007, para 1)

Used across the United States as a freshman convocation and summer reading book, it won many awards including the 2010 *Chicago Tribune* Heartland Prize for Nonfiction, the 2010 Wellcome Trust Book Prize, and the American Association for the Advancement of Science's Award for Excellence in Science Writing, the 2011 Audie Award for Best Non-Fiction Audiobook, and a Medical Journalists' Association Open Book Award.

It's a story inextricably connected to the dark history of experimentation on African Americans, the birth of bioethics, and the legal battles over whether we control the stuff we're made of.

(Skloot, 2017, para. 2)

The compelling story of Henrietta Lacks provides undergraduate researchers an example of why human "subjects" need to be informed, consulted with, and treated fairly when involved in research studies. Even if your study does not involve human subjects, the whole topic of ethics in research methods is something with which you as a researcher should be familiar. Just about every area of research holds some ethical considerations, even if not as directly as the research conducted on Henrietta Lacks.

Research that appears to have absolutely no risk of harm and/or may even benefit participants is not off the hook from informed consent and ethical review. Informed consent means people are agreeing or declining to participate *with full knowledge*, even when there are no known risks either way. Informed consent also includes people agreeing or declining to participate in research that may benefit themselves or others. Why would anyone decide not to answer a short survey for a professor's research if they did not have to provide their name, could take the survey during class time (so would not have to use free time to do so), and would receive extra-credit points for turning it in? The answer is, it doesn't matter. Each of us has the legal right to opt in or out of participating in research without explaining our reasons. Informed consent ensures that people are making the decision with knowledge about what they are agreeing to or declining.

IRB Approval

How do researchers know that they have provided enough information to participants to meet the legal standard of informed consent? How do we guard against unintentionally harmful or ethically questionable research practices? The primary gatekeepers protecting human participants from potential harm or manipulation, and preventing researchers from making ethical or legal violations (even inadvertently), are members of the institutional review board (IRB). Every institution in the U.S. in which research involving humans is conducted—every college and university, research hospital, school district, and other any other type of research facility—has, by law, a committee typically known as the IRB. Other countries have similar ethics boards that go by different names, such as Canada's Tri-Council (made up of representatives of three major granting agencies), the United Kingdom's Research Ethics Committee (REC), and the European Union's Ethics Committee. The 1964 "Declaration of Helsinki" by the World Medical Association established international ethical guidelines for research involving human subjects (World Health Organization, 2001).

According to U.S. federal law, an IRB is made up of at least five experts in biomedical and social-behavioral research ethics. Members of the IRB are charged with protecting the rights and welfare of human subjects/participants in research conducted by anyone affiliated with the institution, including faculty, staff, and students of a college or university. The IRB must review and approve all research involving humans before the research may commence. The chairperson of the IRB is responsible for posting readily accessible (usually online) information about ethical and legal requirements for research involving humans, training sessions for researchers, and the IRB review process.

The IRB review process involves the main researcher, known as the *principal investigator* (PI)—usually the faculty member overseeing the undergraduate research—and the *co-investigator(s)*, who are the student(s) and anyone else collaborating on the research (e.g., community partners or faculty colleagues of the PI). The PI submits the IRB application and is ultimately responsible for ensuring that the research is carried out in accordance with what is described in the application after it has been approved. None of the research involving human subjects/participants can begin before IRB approval—not even recruitment of the participants.

In addition to requiring a description of informed consent, IRB applications call for the following explanations:

- how the PI and co-investigators will protect the privacy and confidentiality of all human participants;
- how the participants will be recruited;
- how the participants will be compensated, if applicable;
- where the participants' confidential and/or identifying information will be stored (e.g., on a password-protected hard drive and/or a locking file cabinet)—and who will have access to it;
- how the PI and co-investigators will dispose of confidential and/or identifying information after the study is complete and a certain period of time has passed (e.g., by fully deleting computer files and shredding paper records); note that IRBs often require the PI to retain records in a secure location for a set period of time, typically three years, after the completion of the study.

If the study includes a survey, a final copy of the survey must be attached. If the study includes interviews, oral histories, and/or focus groups, a list of questions to be asked—often known as the *interview guide* or *protocol*—must be attached. Researchers must stick to the questions on the interview guide, though related follow-up questions are permissible.

The IRB may require revision of the research protocol or even reject the application if required information is missing or incomplete, or if the board determines that the risks of the research are too great. The risks of research are highest when *vulnerable* or *protected populations* are involved; vulnerable populations include children, people in prison, and people with cognitive impairments, to name a few.

Why Is Training on Human Subjects Research Necessary?

Most U.S. college and university IRBs require everyone conducting research with human subjects/participants to complete human-subjects research training every three years. That requirement includes undergraduate researchers. The training is provided by the Collaborative Institutional Training Initiative (CITI), which offers several different online courses and modules. Everyone involved in human-subjects research takes the Responsible Conduct of Research CITI course and/or the Human Subjects Research CITI course, which has a social–behavioral–educational track. Additional modules or courses may be required depending on the nature of the research.

Requiring researchers to take online CITI courses and pass the quizzes helps colleges and universities ensure that research conducted in their name and with their support is done so with ethical integrity. Those who have completed CITI training are much more likely to carry out their research legally and ethically. They are informed about appropriate research protocols and the reasons for particular rules.

Completing training in human-subjects research confers benefits on the researchers themselves, beyond the knowledge they gain about ethical research practices. Practically speaking, completing CITI training dramatically decreases the chance that a researcher will submit an IRB application that gets rejected or requires revision. Having to re-submit an IRB application requires extra time and can cause stress for the researchers. It can significantly delay the start of the study, sometimes for weeks, as protocols need to be rewritten and then reviewed again by the IRB. (At large universities, waiting a month or more for a decision from the IRB is not unusual.) Students working within the confines of a semester have no time to waste. Another benefit of completing CITI training is having ethics course certification among your experiences—a distinctive credential for your résumé and/or graduate-school applications.

How Do I Get Trained?

The IRB chairperson will let the PI know if CITI training is required for the planned research and, if so, which courses need to be taken. Each CITI course takes a few hours but does not need to be completed in one sitting.

If you need to complete CITI training you will not need to pay for the courses. Each college and university has a CITI subscription that covers faculty, staff, and students of the institution.

Before creating an account on the CITI website, find out from the IRB chairperson how your institution handles student registrations and which courses you need to complete. Most likely you will be directed to create an account by entering the name of your institution.

After each course module you will be quizzed on its content. The score considered "passing" is set by the IRB. (At our respective universities the passing score is 80 percent.) Of course, you need a passing score to receive certification of completion.

Questions for Discussion

1   What will happen if I don't take the appropriate steps to protect the rights of participants in my study?
2   How do I know what type of training is necessary?
3   Will CITI training help me after I graduate?
4   How do I choose my participants?

References

Bayer, R. (1995). AIDS, ethics, and activism: Institutional encounters in the epidemic's first decade. In R. E. Bulger, E. M. Bobby, and H. V. Fineberg (eds.), *Society's Choices: Social and Ethical Decision-making in Biomedicine*. Washington, DC: National Academies Press.

De Bord, J. (2014). Informed consent. Ethics in Medicine. Seattle, WA: University of Washington School of Medicine. Retrieved from http://depts.washington.edu/bioethx/topics/consent.html (accessed 14 April 2017).

Skloot, R. (2017). *The Immortal Life of Henrietta Lacks*. New York: Crown Publishing.

World Health Organization. (2001). Declaration of Helsinki. *Bulletin of the World Health Organization*, 79(4), 373–374. Retrieved from www.who.int/bulletin/archives/79(4)373.pdf (accessed 14 April 2017).

5

COLLECTING DATA

In God we trust. All others must bring data.

attributed to W. Edwards Deming

It is a capital mistake to theorize before one has data.

Sir Arthur Conan Doyle, *A Study in Scarlet*

Summary

This chapter explains the importance of sound research methods. It introduces students to qualitative and quantitative methods and when to use one or the other, as well as when to mixed methods. This chapter provides examples of major data-collection strategies for undergraduate research in music, including conducting library research, exploring primary sources, recording one's own observations with research journals and field notes, distributing surveys, and conducting interviews and focus groups. The main differences in methods between arts and humanities scholarship and social science research are described.

Importance of Research Methods

Research is a methodical investigation or inquiry aimed at answering a specific question. The *methodical* approach is what gives a research study rigor and trustworthiness. After learning what is primarily known about the topic area through a review of the literature (see Chapter 2), researchers develop a focused, significant, debatable question (see Chapter 3). As this chapter lays out, researchers then plan their own *methods* for addressing the question. They determine which sources of *data*, or information, would help answer the question and how to access those sources. Purposefully planning methods of data collection and carrying out the research according to that plan (as well as adapting the methods as needed, also based on thoughtful planning) are at the heart of conducting research.

The strength of a research study, therefore, depends most on its *methods*— the processes used to gather data/information to address the research question. Scholars who carefully select the methods best suited to answering the research question set themselves up well for a successful study. A successful study is not necessarily one in which the hypothesis or expected conclusion is proven, but one in which something new and interesting is discovered, and that new and interesting discovery is supported with evidence/data. Sound methods get to that goal.

One of the common missteps we have observed in our mentoring of undergraduate research is a rush to decide on research methods that are obvious and readily accessible. We have had students who tried to rely entirely on secondary sources located through online research, for example, because they were most familiar with that method of information-gathering, even though additional sources of evidence would significantly strengthen their claims. And we have had to guide students away from simply conducting surveys of their peers as their primary research method; although gathering opinions from a group of friends, acquaintances, and/or classmates may be handy, that narrow group of people likely will not provide enough diversity of thought or richness of information to develop a full-fledged conclusion. This chapter is intended to guide student-researchers to more thorough, well-planned methods—methods that are well aligned with the research question and goals of the project.

Sound research methods are critical to the success of your entire study because the results completely depend on the quality of the data, and the quality of the data completely depends on the ways they were collected, recorded, and analyzed. Your process of gathering and analyzing the data must be made evident before your results are presented, in any dissemination of the research, such as a presentation or research paper. The audience's trust in your findings will either be buttressed or undermined by how well you carried out the study and how well you explained the process of carrying it out.

Establishing Credibility as a Researcher

Well-selected research methods—methods chosen precisely because they get at the particular research question—lead to trustworthy results. In addition to setting up a successful study, sound methods give credibility to you as a researcher. For at least 25 centuries of human thought, the credibility of an author has been a foundation of effective argument, or *rhetoric*. In the fourth century BCE, the classical Greek scientist, philosopher, and teacher Aristotle explained that appealing persuasively to an audience requires *logos, pathos,* and *ethos*. Those three parts of a persuasive argument are now known as the *rhetorical triangle*. *Logos* refers literally to the *logic* of one's argument—the reasons, evidence, and explanation that convince others of one's points. *Pathos* concerns appeals to the audience by connecting with them through emotions and values. An example of *pathos* in a research paper about the role of military bands in the U.S. Civil War is the inclusion of a moving story about a particular regiment's band members as a means of connecting readers to a historically distant reality. Statistics can be used as a form of *pathos* as well, such as in a report on the number of high-poverty school districts which have had to eliminate their music programs in the past decade, which may stir audience members' sense of justice and appeal to their values of the arts in public education.

Ethos relates to the character of the writer/speaker. The importance of *ethos* to rhetoric/argument derives from the idea that audience members will only be persuaded by the logic of the claims (*logos*) and the appeals to their values (*pathos*) if they trust the person making the argument. That trust is established when those making claims explain with transparency how they arrived at their conclusions—in the case of research, how they gathered their data and why they went about it in the ways they did. If, on the other hand, the audience is not convinced of the credibility and quality of the work of the researcher, they have no reason to accept the claims.

Triangulated, Intentional, and Impartial Data Collection

Triangulation of Data

Establishing your credibility as a researcher and ensuring, as well as possible, the success of your study requires collecting data in *triangulated, intentional,* and *impartial* ways. *Triangulated data collection* refers to gathering information in a variety of ways as a system of data "checks and balances." Data from one source can be corroborated or disputed by a different source. When multiple sources of information are brought to bear on a research question, the researcher can attain a more reliable and comprehensive understanding. Consider for example a music research study presented by Marie (Terry) Doyon of Bridgewater State University at the 2016 National Conference on Undergraduate Research (NCUR) on European classical vocal pedagogies. As Terry Doyon's abstract explains, she needed to study multiple authors' perspectives on such features as breath support, posture, vocal resonation, and diction in the teaching of singing from the fifteenth to the nineteenth centuries. Pursuing just one or two points of view would be insufficient for understanding the range of pedagogical approaches and their underlying ideologies. Only by culling information from numerous sources and synthesizing it into a multi-faceted claim could she arrive at an informed and insightful argument. That work of drawing from multiple sources is triangulation.

Although the term *triangulation* has led some of our students over the years to conclude that they need exactly three sources of information, the reality is more nuanced than that. The three legs of a simple camp-stool give it stability; take one away, and the stool topples over, but adding legs solidifies it. We prefer to think of triangulation in terms of that metaphorical camp-stool's overall stability rather than its literal three legs. In other words, triangulated research might require only three sources of information to stand solidly on its claims, but it may need more. Would you accept three examples of vocal pedagogy as telling a complete story of European classical styles? If only singular, influential teachers of the late seventeenth century in Germany, Spain, and Italy were studied, would you understand the "European classical world" of vocal pedagogy? What if French vocal teachers of the middle Baroque period, or fifteenth-century composers of the Burgundian school (from present-day France, Belgium, and the Netherlands) were added for consideration? The research would certainly be more thorough and the findings more consequential. Further triangulation could lead to entirely different types of research sources, such as interviews with today's professors of music whose pedagogy is based in some aspects of the classical European schools and/or analysis of archival primary texts, such as journal entries of singers working with various teachers in the seventeenth century describing the abdominal exercises they were given for breath support.

To plan triangulated research methods, you might brainstorm about the various forms of data that could address your research questions (or parts of a single research question) and organize them into a table something like Table 5.1.

Intentionality in Data Collection

Lest it sound as if more and more sources automatically make research better, we move to the second criterion of sound research methods: intentionality.

TABLE 5.1 Planning triangulated methods

Part 1 of research question	First method of data collection for question 1	Second method of data collection for question 1	Third method of data collection for question 1
Part 2 of research question	First method of data collection for question 2	Second method of data collection for question 2	Third method of data collection for question 2

Intentional data collection refers to the careful thinking involved in determining which sources to pursue. What types of data will allow you to gain the information you need? By selecting sources of information intentionally and then explaining why you collected data in the ways you did, you avoid a scattershot (random and overly general) approach to research. In Terry Doyon's study of European classical vocal pedagogies, for instance, her intentionality led to choosing salient examples of teaching methods that were most influential in the shift in Europe from Catholic Church monastic singing to the development of the opera. Simply compiling example after example of famous vocal teachers would not have been nearly as effective as selecting the key innovators who changed the world of vocal education. Intentionally pairing up the teachers' pedagogical philosophies with journal entries of their best-known students made for an even more compelling study.

Avoiding Bias and Ensuring Impartiality

The third expectation of credible researchers, *impartiality*, requires effort to reduce potential bias and errors. Biased or otherwise sloppy scholarship undermines the study itself as well as the credibility of the researcher. Bias in research comes in many forms, some of it unconscious on the part of the researcher. It might include preference for, or prejudice against, a particular outcome that leads to overemphasis (or ignoring) of certain results. If a researcher expects members of a focus group to be enthusiastic about a shared experience, the researcher might glom on to a few stray comments that fit that expectation. On the flip side, if members of the focus group suspect the researcher is hoping for particular responses, they might accommodate that expectation, especially if they have a relationship with the researcher that would benefit from positive reinforcement. For those very reasons the best practices of focus-group research include having a neutral person facilitate and record the discussion, without the researcher even in the room.

Similarly, the ways in which survey questions are worded may reveal the biases of the researcher and skew responses. Using validated survey instruments designed by researchers with expertise in survey design mitigates those tendencies toward unconscious bias. If you need to develop your own survey, we recommend studying the elements of good design, starting with guidelines for beginning survey researchers, such as Vannette's (2015) "10 Tips for Building Effective Surveys" and asking for feedback on your draft questions from professors who teach research methods.

Even peer-reviewed research articles are likely to reflect the values of the journals that publish them, so over-reliance on sources from one journal should be avoided. As these examples indicate, impartial research design requires vigilance. Consistently asking yourself how sources of data could be obtained with the least possibility for bias can lead to helpful ideas for fair and even-handed methods. Explaining in your method section the steps you took to reduce bias and the chance of errors demonstrates your impartiality and credibility as a researcher. Informed readers can and should be attentive to signs of prejudice and imprecision in reports of research. They will appreciate indications that you collected data carefully and as impartially as possible.

Quantitative, Qualitative, and Mixed Methods Research

How do you decide on the types of research data to triangulate, select intentionally, and collect impartially? One rough breakdown of the types of research data you might gather is *quantitative* and *qualitative*. *Quantitative data* is numerically measurable and reportable information. Quantitative data literally show the calculable quantity or amount of something. Examples include the number or percentage of participants who gave a particular response to a survey question; the average increase in scores between participants' pre-test and post-test; the amount of time needed to complete a series of tasks; and even the results of a structural analysis of the complexity of a piece of music.

Qualitative data cannot be measured numerically; it is descriptive information about the qualities of people's ideas or behaviors, or any other subject of study that requires interpretation rather than calculation. Examples of qualitative data include transcripts of interviews; open-ended written responses on surveys; analysis of the emotions expressed in a piece of music; observations of people's behaviors described in field notes; and evaluations of body language, tone of voice, and/or word choices.

Sources of information are rarely exclusively quantitative or qualitative; many can be analyzed in different ways for quantitative or qualitative data, such as pre-tests and post-tests that could be evaluated in terms of how many responses were correct (quantitative measure) and/or analyzed for patterns in the open-ended responses (qualitative interpretation). Likewise, researchers often benefit from obtaining both quantitative and qualitative data. Using both types of information to get at different facets of the research question is known as *mixed methods research*.

Quantitative Methods

The following are the most common quantitative methods used by undergraduate researchers in music.

- *Surveys/questionnaires with multiple-choice or Likert-scale responses*: Surveys and questionnaires capture demographic and/or opinion data that are self-reported by individuals. A Likert scale is usually made up of five or seven choices aimed at measuring degrees of agreement, from strongly disagree to strongly agree, for example. A Likert scale provides a more nuanced set of responses than simple agree-or-disagree binary choices.

• *Tests of content knowledge, ability, attitude, or skill:* Pre-test and post-test data are often used to determine whether an intervention, such as a new teaching technique or a particular experience or event, may have affected participants' knowledge or attitudes. The pre-test and post-test ask for the same information at different points in time—days, weeks, or months apart. pre-tests and post-tests may be given to one group of participants to measure change over time, or distributed to two sets of participants known as the *experimental group* and *control group* in order to make a comparison between them. The experimental group participates in the intervention being studied ("the experiment"), such as a new method of teaching. The control group continues with the status quo. Experimental and control groups usually share basic demographics in common. A study aimed at determining whether *flipped classroom* techniques would improve learning outcomes in a high-school advanced placement (AP) music theory class could employ flipped classroom techniques with one AP class (the experimental group) while the other AP class would learn the content the same way it traditionally has been taught (the control group). In a flipped classroom, content that is usually delivered in lectures in class is now accessed by students outside of class, as homework. In-class time is repurposed for active and experiential learning; students apply the information they read or watched in video-recorded lectures outside of class to collaborative, inquiry-based projects during class.

• *Structural analysis of music or other texts:* A quantitative structural analysis entails some form of counting, such as the number of a type of time signature in a composer's work or the words that came up most frequently on an online discussion board.

• *Statistical analysis:* The analysis of statistical data gathered by oneself or previous researchers is a sophisticated quantitative research skill. Statistical data include a vast array of evidence, from individuals' personal/demographic information to immense sets of organizational and national information.

Qualitative Methods

These are the most common forms of qualitative data in undergraduate research in music:

• *Surveys/questionnaires with open-response questions:* Open-response questions invite survey-takers to write out answers to questions that do not lend themselves to either-or or multiple-choice responses. They allow participants to convey a range of ideas, attitudes, and examples, often providing rich information for researchers. (Many surveys of course include both quantitative and qualitative questions.)

- *Interviews.* Interviews, which are typically one-on-one interactions in which the participant answers a set of questions posed by the researcher/interviewer, may be audio-recorded with the permission of the participant. Whether the interview is recorded or not, the interviewer usually takes extensive notes during and immediately following the interview.
- *Focus groups.* Focus groups are akin to group interviews. A group of people with something in common that is of interest to the researcher (e.g., students in a summer undergraduate-research program; attendees of the same concert; survey respondents who checked the box at the end of the survey indicating their willingness to be contacted for follow-up research) is invited to participate in a discussion about the topic. The group should be small enough that everyone can contribute a response to some or all of the questions —usually between 5 and 20 participants. The facilitator poses questions to the group and may either encourage a free exchange of responses or suggest a means of equitable participation. Focus groups may be audio-recorded with the informed consent of each participant. Sometimes a note-taker accompanies the facilitator so that the facilitator can attend to the group dynamics without the additional task of writing notes.
- *Document analysis:* Some student-researchers get the extraordinary opportunity to work with primary sources in an archive or much more accessible online collection. *Primary sources* are original documents or artifacts created in the time period being studied, such as diaries/journals, original manuscripts and composition notes, letters and other correspondence, and audio and video recordings. Archives around the world preserve original documents of historical and cultural significance in secure, fire-proof cabinets in temperature-controlled, low-humidity rooms, all to ensure that they will not be lost to current and future generations. University library archives, as well as many archives associated with museums, historical societies, and other public and private libraries, offer rich troves of primary sources for student-researchers. You may be required to get a brief training from the archivist and to wear archivist gloves—or you may have to view fragile, high-value pieces through plastic or glass—but those precautions are well worthwhile, as there is nothing quite like the thrill of working with a document written in a world-famous musician's own hand. Digitized library and museum collections have made primary-source research possible from your own computer or your university's library database. Digital photos of documents and recordings of sound bring the archives right to you. Anything that interprets or is otherwise at a remove from a primary text (e.g., an article that includes excerpts of letters) is a *secondary*

source. Your notes in a research journal—capturing key quotations as well as your own textual analysis and observations—are invaluable sources of qualitative data. When reading and analyzing a text (whether in the form of music, a narrative text, a data table, or a piece of artwork, to name a few), you could be jotting down ideas that strike you, direct quotations you want to use and cite, questions that pop up in your mind, connections you see to other texts, and any number of other thoughts. The process of taking those notes, especially if you color-code them according to patterns and/or mark up significant details, is a form of qualitative data analysis.

- *Case study*: Empirical observation and analysis of one important case (or small number of cases) may give deep insight into a broader issue. The "case" may be a person, course, event, or other phenomenon. Jiaying (Iris) Zhu's 2014 NCUR presentation on Chinese composers who broke with tradition and worked in Western musical styles, derived from case studies of three composers, each in a different time period: He Luting, Li Yinghai, and Tan Dun. In analyzing each case, such as He Luting being forced to hide his work during the Chinese Cultural Revolution at the risk of imprisonment and even execution for "treason," Zhu was able to make a larger assertion about the evolution of Western musical styles in China.

- *Observation* (also called *field observation* or *direct observation*): Conducting observations on behaviors or other phenomena in a certain setting can be a valuable qualitative research method when carried out by rigorous researchers who are doing much more than simply watching. Observation research requires detailed field notes about what is observed—a crucial aspect of its methodological rigor. Sometimes the field notes are structured to include certain behaviors or participants while purposely ignoring others in order to focus on a predetermined set of data, such as observation research on orchestra cello players. Other field notes are open to everything that catches the researcher's attention, without a prediction of what to expect. If the observation is to be conducted covertly (without the knowledge and consent of those being observed), privacy must be protected, and the IRB will consider whether the research could be conducted effectively with informed participants instead. If the subjects/participants know they are being observed, the researcher must consider the Hawthorne Effect, the psychological phenomenon of people changing their behavior because they are being observed. Such decisions about covert or overt observations are usually discussed in the method section of a research paper.

- *Participant observation*: Conducting observations on the behaviors of a group of people while involved with them over a period of time offers a more intimate angle on observation research. Examples of participant observation include student-teachers conducting research on student learning in their lead teachers' classrooms; a member of a string quartet seeking to determine the most effectual practice techniques for small groups of musicians; and undergraduate researchers in music reflecting on their own and their classmates' experiences in their capstone class as a means of informing future students, as they have done for this book. Like other forms of observation, participant observation requires detailed field notes, though the notes may have to be written immediately after the observation time because participating and note-taking simultaneously may not be possible.

Some forms of research can be quantitative, qualitative, or mixed methods, depending on the types of information to be gathered. Two examples are:

- *Longitudinal study*: Empirical observation and analysis of something over a significant period of time (e.g., ten-year commitment to playing an instrument after a particular form of instruction).
- *Pilot study*: Collecting data about a new intervention or process while it is carried out for the first time, and analyzing the data to determine the intervention's longer term efficacy.

Note that IRB approval is required for all of these forms of research except when they do not involve people in any way. IRB approval is not required for use of *archival data*—information already collected by other researchers (who had IRB approval) that is now available, with no personally identifiable information, for new researchers to analyze.

Arts and Humanities Methods

You may notice that in some scholarly papers in the arts and humanities, research methods are discussed only briefly or may even be implicit (not explicitly identified). That occurs when the author is using a widely accepted method with which the intended audience would be familiar. An ethnographic study published in a journal dedicated to ethnography, for example, would omit some of the rationale for the selected method. For undergraduate research papers and presentations, however, the method should be made apparent, as the audience is rarely limited to narrow experts.

That said, you may also notice explanations of scholarly processes that are referred to in other terms. Many scholars in the arts and humanities would not use the word *method* to describe their process of collecting information, as it is traditionally associated with research that is *empirical* (verifiable by observation) or *experimental* (based on scientific tests). Much of the scholarly work conducted in the arts and humanities is *theoretical*: it builds on existing knowledge to explain or create new concepts/phenomena. Theoretical scholarship is distinct from empirical and experimental research in many ways, as indicated by the different terminology.

One of our students, for example, did an undergraduate research project that consisted of setting several Anne Bradstreet poems as songs for a solo mezzo-soprano voice with piano accompaniment. Her work was theoretical as well as creative because it built on existing knowledge of how to compose musical phrases to create new songs for a particular voice range. It also built on existing poetic works to generate a new form for Bradstreet's words.

Scholars doing theoretical and creative work may or may not use the term *method* to describe their process. Alternative terms include *process, technique, approach* (including *theoretical approach* and *critical approach*), *study,* and *analysis*. The student who set Bradstreet poems as songs for mezzo-soprano explained her "scholarly process" rather than her "research methods" because that terminology fitted her work better. All of that is to say that various terms may be used in different contexts, but whatever phrasing is used, scholars are expected to describe the methods of their inquiries. In that student's case, she explained several parts of her scholarly process:

- creating each musical phrase in correspondence with a line of text by using compositional techniques such as *word painting* (or *tone painting*)–writing music that matches the literal meaning of the words of a song;
- after developing each melody with pitches within the range of mezzo-sopranos, writing the piano accompaniment using traditional harmony, with melodic independence for solo lines—mostly major or minor keys, with sporadic modes for color;
- writing in smaller musical details, including dynamic markings and articulations;
- programming the compositions, which were drafted on staff paper, into a musical notation program.

Those methods align with the student's goals for the project and demonstrate that she possesses the knowledge and ability to do the work.

Social Science Methods

Some scholarship in the field of music, such as research in music education and music therapy, would be characterized as social science research, which is mainly *empirical* (verifiable by observation), though social scientists also conduct theoretical research. One of our students majoring in music education conducted a research study during his student-teaching semester in a middle-school band class. He hypothesized that sixth-graders who had band as their first-period class would be more alert and therefore more successful on exams in their second-period class than students whose band class was after lunch. The student's methods were *empirical* in that he could answer his research question mainly through observation of the sixth-graders' exam scores and self-reports of their alertness. His empirical methods included the following steps:

- developing pre-tests and post-tests of alertness based on models in the research literature;
- working with his faculty mentor to complete the university's IRB application for ethics review (see Chapter 4);
- obtaining informed consent of parents for their minor children to participate in the research study;
- distributing, recording, and analyzing student responses to pre-tests and post-tests of alertness before and after first-period classes—for both groups of students (those who had band class in their first period, and those who had it after lunch);
- with the permission of the school principal and participating teachers, analyzing exam scores (without any identifying information) across multiple second-period sixth-grade classes.

As you can see in a comparison of the two students' main methods (setting poems to songs for mezzo-soprano and studying effects of early-morning music-playing on alertness and grades), each pursued a very different means of answering their research questions in the field of music—just as each ought to. The student-teacher's question required an empirical approach that obviously would not work for a theoretical/creative project.

That study of the effects of first-period band on middle-school students' academic performance in the second hour of their day might also draw on theory, though, in which case the methods would include *theoretical* as well as empirical research. The student could analyze theories about the effects of music on the brain and draw connections to his own study. Building on existing knowledge about music-playing affecting the brain would be a theoretical method.

Another way that social scientists conduct theoretical research is in the reverse order: rather than analyzing an existing theory and applying it to one's own work, researchers sometimes develop a new theory from their research findings. The term for that form of research is *grounded theory*. The new theory emerges from the "ground" up. A scholar may discover something through empirical research that is not explainable with existing theories. The discovery could be a fluke or a simple anomaly. But if the discovery can be replicated in a different context or otherwise leads to a new understanding, the researcher might develop a grounded theory.

Organizing the Method Section of a Research Paper

The scholarly methods or processes are usually explained in a paper after the introduction and the review of the literature. Many professors, journal editors, and other readers of your written work, especially in the social sciences, expect research papers to follow a standard format:

1 *Abstract*, a brief overview (anywhere from 60–250 words, depending on the particular guidelines provided) of the whole paper, with a focus on the methods, results, and implications of the research.
2 *Introduction*, the purposes of which are to orient readers to the topic of inquiry and inspire interest in it.
3 *Literature Review*.
4 *Method*.
5 *Results*.
6 *Discussion*.
7 *Conclusion*, which typically offers next steps and implications of the research.

Academic posters often include each of those sections as well, though the order may be moved around as needed for column space and visual appeal. Oral presentations may also cue the audience when moving to each section, to clarify distinctions between what came from the review of the literature, for example, as opposed to what was learned in the speaker's own research study.

Subsections of the Method Section

Within each of those sections researchers usually include *subsections* to delineate and organize further the points that go together within each section. Subsections are particularly helpful to aid the reader's understanding of long research papers. We focus here on typical subsections of a method section. The subsections of a literature review (see Chapter 2) and results and discussion sections (see Chapter 6) are unique to each paper because they emerge from the themes of the particular research study.

The method section of a research paper or poster, however, often includes three standard subsections, organized under their own subheadings:

Participants

A description of the human subjects/participants involved in the study and how they were recruited or observed, if applicable. In most cases, participants should not be identifiable. Typical information to provide about participants:

- number of participants, which may include the number recruited as well as how many actually participated, if applicable;
- gender breakdown;
- race and ethnicity breakdown;
- range of ages and median age.

Information particular to your participants should be included as well; e.g., "All participants were undergraduate students at a large public university in the southeastern United States."

This subsection could also describe briefly how participants were recruited; e.g., "Potential interview subjects were recruited by email, using contact information provided in the National Music Educators directory. The recruitment email introduced the researcher, summarized the purpose of the study, noted the university's IRB approval, and requested 30 minutes of the participant's time for an interview over Skype."

Materials

Information about the things used to collect data and/or conduct measurements (e.g., surveys, timed tests, materials the participants read or listened to). This subsection is termed *Apparatus* when the data were gathered through the use of technical equipment or research instruments (e.g., noise-canceling headphones, eye-movement tracking device, analytical software) or *Apparatus and Materials* if a mixture of mechanisms were used to collect data. Please note that this subsection may need a different subheading that more accurately captures what kinds of things were used to obtain information (e.g., *Survey Instrument* may be a better subheading than *Materials* if the only research material was a survey).

Procedure

An explanation of how the data were collected, verified, and analyzed. The procedure section usually includes a discussion of *variables*, or factors that can change and therefore could affect the results of the study. Consider for example a study of how listening to symphonic music composed by Mozart while studying for Calculus I exams might affect student performance on the exams. There are multiple variables to consider in such a study: how long each participant studied; what times of day/night the studying took place; participants' studying environments and conditions; etc. Rigorous research attempts to control for as many variables as possible, such as by selecting participants with similar study habits and similar grades on previous exams. Any such attempts to limit the number of variables should be noted. Explain the variables that could not be controlled (e.g., participants' studying environments) and acknowledge how they could affect the results.

Variables that may weaken the results of the study are a form of *Limitations*. The limitations of your research methods should be acknowledged either as you discuss each method or in summary at the end of the method section.

While those three subsections are fairly standard, students are often not required to include them in exactly that way, nor to be limited to those three. In a paper on a complex research study, additional subsections are often needed to delineate aspects of the research methods.

Our students often ask us how much detail is needed in the method section. As you can imagine, anyone who has conducted a long, complicated research project could go on and on about each step of the process, but an exhaustive account would not be of interest or need to most audiences. A widely accepted consideration for the degree of detail in a method section is whether future researchers would have enough information to replicate the study in their own settings. One aspect of research is the reliability of results: the extent to which the results would be consistent if the study were carried out again with similar conditions. Reliability can only be tested if each researcher's methods are spelled out with enough clarity for others to run the investigation again. We recommend trying to strike a balance between presenting clear, replicable information about stages of your research process and not going into excruciating detail. Reading method sections of published papers in your topic area is the best way of understanding where that balance lies.

More about Acknowledging the Limitations of the Research

Every research study has certain limitations: it is limited by the number of survey respondents, or the amount of time over which a change is studied, or the inherent bias of the researcher, just to name a few examples. Some limitations are unavoidable and expected.

When the limitations will undermine the results of your research, however, you need to use an alternative method of data collection. If the student-teacher studying first-period band students were to receive informed consent from only a small percentage of parents of students in the class, he would need to adjust his methods or add another form of data collection for triangulation. When the limitations are avoidable (such as when your presence in a focus group could prompt less-than-honest responses, and someone else could facilitate the focus group instead), you are expected to do your best to prevent them.

Unavoidable limitations that you anticipate ahead of time should be noted in the method section. What are the limitations in each form of data you are collecting? For example, were you only able to study one group of people (an experimental group) without a control group for comparison? Were there distortions in the digital sound recording you analyzed? Was the single semester you had for your capstone project an insufficient amount of time to measure significant differences in pre-tests and post-tests? There is no need to document each and every imperfection in your research process; only the factors that likely weakened the project in noticeable ways need to be acknowledged. Later, when you discuss the results (see Chapter 6) you can speculate on how some results may have been affected by the limitations.

Other Means of Organizing Research Methods

Earlier in this chapter we noted that various disciplines use different terms for *methods*, as well as different ways of organizing scholarly writing. Those differences are not arbitrary or accidental, of course. Each academic discipline is distinguished by its *epistemology*, or its theories and ways of knowing. Epistemology encompasses why and how people in a particular field of study gain knowledge: how we know what we know, which methods are used to teach and discover knowledge, which forms of evidence are considered valid, where knowledge originates, and where its limits might be. It stands to reason that scholars operating under different epistemologies would pursue new knowledge in divergent ways and therefore write and speak about their processes in divergent ways.

A good example of the different terminology reflecting different epistemologies is the word "procedure," which is particularly suited to empirical and experimental research. Scholars making empirical observations or running experiments must take great care with their research protocol, or procedure. To guard against bias in their observations, to measure accurately, to make equal comparisons, and for many other reasons, empirical and experimental researchers need to follow established procedures. They know that their results will only be meaningful if their data are collected and recorded in precise, methodical steps. Detailing their procedure in the method section of a research paper is understandably expected.

The procedures followed by theoretical and creative scholars are not usually so rigorous or clear-cut—nor do they need to be. A great deal of the scholarly work done in the arts and humanities is interpretive. There is no single, established procedure for analyzing a piece of music, much less for composing one! Individual scholars take their own approaches to theoretical and creative projects, and those approaches are not necessarily linear or prescriptive. Creative projects in the arts, as well as many other fields, are notoriously ill-structured. We know a scholar of "pure mathematics" who studies concepts so abstract they have no real-world referents; when asked to describe her methods of constructing proofs she said simply, "I think about the problem for a really long time." Imagine explaining the procedure for that research method!

Students conducting scholarly work that does not fit the methods and terminology of empirical or experimental research have an array of options for describing their processes, including the following two, which could also serve as subheadings:

- *Research design*: A summary of the investigation (the research question/ goal and a few objectives of the study) and the major stages of gathering information to address the question/goal. The stages of information-gathering may be organized *chronologically* (starting with the first step and concluding with the last) or *thematically* (clustering related steps together).
- *Theoretical approach* (also called *critical approach* or *methodological approach*): An explanation of the theory or theories that were foundational to the research and how that existing theory was applied to your own study. We recommend starting by summarizing the theory and then demonstrating its relevance to your research question. A theoretical idea may be used as a kind of lens for examining primary or secondary sources or other qualitative data; it may offer a methodological approach that you can adapt for your own investigation; and/or a theory may be brought into dialogue with other theories to create a richer understanding of the topic of study.

Questions for Discussion

1   Are there standard ways to collect data?
2   Which data collection methods are appropriate for my topic?
3   How do I judge whether my sample size is appropriate?

References

Vannette, D. (2015). 10 tips for building effective surveys. Qualtrics. Retrieved from www.qualtrics.com/blog/10-tips-for-building-effective-surveys/ (accessed 14 April 2017).

6

ANALYZING AND SYNTHESIZING DATA

Analysis and synthesis are different mental muscles to serve different purposes.
Pearl Zhu, *Thinkingaire*

Analysis is the art of creation through destruction.
P. S. Baber, *Cassie Draws the Universe*

Summary

The results or findings are the most substantive part of conducting research. This chapter outlines how research results and interpretation of those results are reported in different disciplines and types of papers and presentations. It provides prompts for freewriting or otherwise thinking about the implications of data. While a full exploration of qualitative and quantitative data analysis is beyond the scope of this text, this chapter includes fundamental information about the terms and techniques involved in analyzing different types of information. It discusses the importance of triangulating results, identifying overarching themes, and aligning the discussion of research results with the research question and the review of the literature. The chapter concludes with a reminder about acknowledging any limitations of the research that significantly affect the results.

Results and Discussion

The *results* (or *findings*) of your study constitute what you have learned from the research process. The results include the data along with your analysis or interpretation of the data. Merely reporting the data is not enough. The point of research is the *analysis* and *interpretation* of what the data signify.

In most reports of scholarly work the results/findings are explained right after the methods/process. In APA-style, social-science papers, the *results* are reported separately from the *discussion*. The results section gives a basic explanation of the data, and the subsequent discussion section provides more thorough interpretation of the results and explains the wider implications of what was discovered. In papers and presentations in the arts and humanities, however, the results or findings are usually interpreted while they are reported. There is no divide between the results and discussion—or between the results and the researcher's interpretation and statement of implications.

Analyzing Research Data

Knowing the etymology (origin) of the verb *analyze* can be a useful means of understanding what is really called for when you are asked to analyze information. The Latin origin of *analysis* translates to the "resolution of anything complex into simple elements" (Online Etymology Dictionary, n.d.). In that original concept of analysis as the breaking down of complex ideas, analysis is posited as the opposite of *synthesis*, which refers to putting parts back into a coherent whole. That idea effectively informs the task of data analysis, which is very much about breaking apart complex information into simpler parts. The Greek etymology of *analysis* adds another facet to this understanding: "a breaking up, a loosening, releasing"; the verb form in Greek is "to set free; to loose a ship from its moorings" (Online Etymology Dictionary, n.d.). Imagine for a moment what that version of analysis might look like in undergraduate research. What would it mean to "loosen" or "release" research data? How does the image of a ship set free of its moorings represent something about the task of analyzing information? We see the work of data analysis as analogous to the Latin and Greek origins of the English word. Analysis is an act of setting free into the world the knowledge contained in quantitative and qualitative data. The analyzer's work of breaking the data apart helps others make sense of the information. The researcher's analysis could even be described as loosening up the densely packed evidence, allowing others to see and understand the component parts.

Analysis is what gives meaning to the quantitative and qualitative data you have collected. The data do not hold meaning in and of themselves; it is your analytical work that translates for others what the information actually signifies. This chapter offers tools and techniques for doing that important work of making meaning from data.

Data Analysis Exercise

Examine each piece of data you have collected and freewrite answers to the following questions:

- What is interesting/exciting/notable about this piece of information?
- What is the story it can tell?
- Do you think this data-point misrepresents what is really going on?
- What, if anything, is disappointing about it?
- Is it consistent with anything you found in your review of the literature? Does it contradict anything you read in the research literature?
- How could it be most effectively presented? In narrative form? In tables or graphs? Key quotations? (Quotations may come from textual analysis, from research participants, from your own research journal, etc.)

Identifying Themes in the Data

The analysis of data is about figuring out the *implications* (or conclusions that can be drawn) of what was discovered. To help our students start to organize their research results we ask them to list and then freewrite about three to five themes they have learned from their research (the implications). The next step is to compose a topic sentence for each of those themes: a specific, clear, supportable claim about what the data indicate.

We recommend going from there (composing topic sentences on a few clear themes) to organizing data around each of those topic sentences—perhaps by creating an outline or flow chart. Structure the outline by those topic sentences rather than by each piece of data. This is important: the data do not organize themselves. You as the researcher are the agent. You decide the ordering of points, and you plug in the data as evidence for those points. We have seen it go the wrong way too many times: the surveys say *a*, the primary sources say *b* and *c*, and many of the secondary sources seem to corroborate the survey respondents (*a*), but a few others say something entirely different (*d* and *e*). When research reports are organized by the data they are messy and confusing, whipping around from one piece of evidence to the next without a sense of control or clear meaning. Successful researchers analyze the data first to identify the implications/themes. The implications of the research are the most interesting points. Then researchers figure out which pieces of data support each of those implications. The difference is enormous between listing a bunch of data that needs to be made sense of and stating clear, focused claims backed up by data.

The data may be represented as evidence in many different forms, including textual evidence (quotations and paraphrases); quotations from survey responses, interviews, or focus groups; and/or tables or graphs of quantitative data. However the data are represented, remember that they play a supporting role. They are the back-up to the claims you make.

Analyzing Quantitative Data

A full explanation of how to analyze quantitative data is beyond the scope of this book. Students who have taken a course in quantitative research methods may be able to conduct a *multivariate analysis* of their data, which involves the examination of multiple variables in the data in relationship to one another (e.g., correlations among 300 college-student participants' ages, genders, years of playing an instrument, and number of minutes spent practicing per week). However, that level of analysis requires statistical calculation skills that are not typically expected in the field of music. This discussion sticks to the terms and types of calculations involved in *univariate* (single variable) and *bivariate* (two variables in interaction with each other) quantitative analysis.

If your research involves a quantitative survey, questionnaire, and/or tests, you have an array of software platforms for building the research instrument, distributing it, collecting data, and even doing preliminary analysis. Platforms such as Survey Monkey, Wufoo, and Qualtrics generate reports and allow users to download data in order to create customized spreadsheets and conduct analysis. While those user-friendly ways of reporting data help even those without statistical training to capture and compare data, the researcher's own analysis is needed to explain the relationships within and significance of the information. The following explanations are intended to guide that analysis with regard to fundamental quantitative data. The terms used here apply to most types of quantitative data, including those discussed in Chapter 5: surveys/questionnaires; pre- and post-tests; structural analysis; and statistical analysis.

Correlation

Correlation is the relationship between two or more data points, such that when one piece of data changes for a certain sample of the population, the other changes too—either in the same or opposite direction. For example, there is a statistical correlation, or relationship, between the highest level of education a group of people have completed and their income levels. There is also a correlation/relationship (though in the opposite direction) between a population's highest level of education completed and their rates of cigarette smoking. Correlation is not the same as *causation*. Correlation indicates that a relationship exists but does not on its own show that one thing caused the other.

Direct Correlation/Positive Correlation/Direct Relationship

These three interchangeable terms all refer to a "positive" relationship between two or more data points. A positive relationship means that when one data point increases, the other does too; when one decreases, so does the other. In the example in the previous paragraph, a population's highest level of education completed and their income levels have a positive correlation or direct relationship, according to many studies. When one is high, the other tends to be too; when one is low, the other usually is as well. What other variables would you expect to have a positive correlation with highest level of education completed? The number of books read in the last year? Likelihood of living in urban areas?

Inverse Correlation/Negative Correlation/Inverse Relationship

These interchangeable terms all indicate an inverse or negative correlation between two or more data points; the data points go in opposite directions when there is a negative correlation. When one increases, the other tends to decrease, and vice versa. Using the same example set above, one would see in many studies that highest education completed tends to have an inverse relationship with rates of cigarette smoking. In other words, the more education a person completes, the less likely that person is to smoke cigarettes on a regular basis. The negative correlation occurs the opposite way too: someone who smokes cigarettes frequently is less likely to have completed college. In other words, the more education a person completes, the less likely that person is to smoke cigarettes on a regular basis. The negative correlation occurs the opposite way too: someone who smokes cigarettes frequently is less likely to have completed college. Can you identify some other negative correlations with highest level of education completed? How about the likelihood of believing conspiracy theories? The number of children they have?

Frequency Distribution

A frequency distribution is a display of how often (how frequently) members of a particular population sample gave particular responses (or did particular behaviors or said particular words). A frequency distribution table shows how many participants gave each response (on a survey or test question) or how many times a phenomenon occurred (in a structural analysis).   •

For the purposes of defining some key terms, consider a survey of 300 music students that includes the question, *How many years have you been playing a musical instrument?* The multiple-choice options are (a) less than 2 years, (b) 2–3 years, (c) 4–6 years, (d) 7–10 years, and (e) more than 10 years. Table 6.1 outlines the responses based on gender identity.

TABLE 6.1 Length of time playing a musical instrument, by gender identity

Gender identity	Less than 2 years	2–3 years	4–6 years	7–10 years	More than 10 years	Total
Female	11	17	29	43	82	182
Male	8	18	14	30	35	105
Other or prefer not to answer	2	0	5	2	4	13
Total	21	35	48	75	121	300

TABLE 6.2 10 years or more of playing an instrument, by gender identity

Gender identity	Frequency	Percent
Female	82	68%
Male	35	29%
Other or prefer not to answer	4	3%
Total	121	100%

Table 6.2 shows the *frequency distribution* by gender of the particular response (e) 10 years or more. The frequency distribution of male students who reported playing an instrument for 10 years or more is 35. These data could be used for a bivariate analysis of gender identity correlated with years of playing an instrument.

Basic Statistical Terms

- *Mean*: Average of all the scores (using the mean has drawbacks when there are extreme or outlier scores, which skew the mean).
- *Median:* The middle score when all responses are ranked.
- *Mode:* The most frequently occurring score or phenomenon.
- *Range:* The difference between the highest and lowest responses.
- *Standard Deviation*: How much participants' scores differ from the mean (average) score (i.e., the deviation of each score from the mean/average).

Structural Analysis in Music

An example of a quantitative structural analysis in music is a study of tempi of two famous conductors' recordings of Brahms' Symphony no. 1 with the Berlin Philharmonic, about 20 years apart (though with many of the same musicians). Tempo measurements were recorded and displayed in a comprehensive table of measurements so that the reader could easily see the biggest disparities. The undergraduate researcher then compared the tempo measurements with subjective annotations about why the conductors might have chosen those tempi. The quantitative data (tempo measurements) were not meaningful on their own. It was the student's analysis of the conductors' choices that illuminated the information and allowed him to put forth an interesting set of conclusions about the decisions of different conductors with regard to the same piece of music and when working with many of the same musicians.

Analyzing Qualitative Data

The metaphor of unpacking luggage is an apt description of how to analyze qualitative data, including primary and secondary source texts, research-journal notes, participant responses (from open-response survey questions, interviews, or focus groups), and any other information that cannot be quantified. Imagine taking each piece of qualitative data, one by one, out of its place and holding it up for examination. What is interesting about it? How is it different from the other things (the other data points) right next to it? With what else does it logically go? Asking and answering those kinds of questions about qualitative data help bring the information to life, in a way. Thinking about the interesting qualities of each piece of data helps you to put together a meaningful story from your own interpretation of the data.

Coding

An example of qualitative data analysis comes from a student who conducted focus groups with undergraduate music majors who participated in an after-school music mentoring program for middle-school band students. The student-researcher asked open-ended questions about the efficacy of the program and its potential benefits for both mentors and mentees, recorded the responses, and transcribed them. The student's transcription of the responses was only the first step of data analysis. Next, she examined the transcript for patterns. Every time the idea of "giving back" or "paying forward" came up in the participants' responses, she highlighted the text in yellow. When participants described positive relationships with their mentees, the comments were highlighted in blue. Comments about the mentors improving their own music practice as a result of their mentoring work were highlighted in green. Indications of frustration with the mentees' lack of commitment were highlighted in pink, etc. Then, examining a multi-colored transcript of the focus group discussion, the student-researcher could identify some prominent themes—namely that the mentors mentioned rewards nearly three times as often as frustrations or difficulties, and that the most frequently mentioned rewards were a sense of satisfaction in giving back to the community and appreciation for their relationships with mentees.

That form of qualitative data analysis is known as *coding*. Similar data—or pieces of data that share the same idea—are coded by theme. The coding can be done by hand on hard copies using colored highlighters or annotations by pen or pencil (e.g., asterisk as one code, check-mark as another, etc.) or on the computer using the highlighter function in word-processing programs. For large data sets, coding can be done using analytical software (e.g., SPSS, Nvivo, Dedoose) that organizes pieces of text by code/theme.

Limitations of the Research

As explained in Chapter 5, every research study has certain limitations. Every researcher is limited by time, resources, access to information, etc. When the limitations of the study significantly affects results, researchers need to identify the issue and explain the ramifications. What if, for example, a student studying a lesser-known but important composer discovered in the course of the research that primary sources and other archival materials about the composer were less informative than the student first thought they would be? Not all would be lost, especially if the composer's musical works were available for analysis; but the influences from the composer's personal relationships, thought to factor into her work, could not be fairly determined from the few journal entries and letters that survive. That lack of information and its impact on the research should be noted and discussed.

Questions for Discussion

1 Are you most drawn to qualitative or quantitative analysis?
2 What about mixed-methods research?
3 What happens when the results are not what you expected?

Reference

Online Etymology Dictionary. (n.d.). Analysis. Retrieved from www.etymonline.com/index.php?allowed_in_frame=0&search=analysis (accessed 14 April 2017).

7

CITING SOURCES

People seldom improve when they have no model but themselves to copy after.
Oliver Goldsmith, *On Our Theatres*

I get a lot of big ideas, and occasionally I actually come up with one myself.
M. C. Humphreys, *Some Inspiration for the Overenthusiastic*

Summary

Responsible scholars give credit to other researchers and authors by correctly acknowledging ideas that are not their own. Giving credit is accomplished through the use of citations and bibliographies. This chapter discusses MLA and APA guidelines as well as some of the reasons for using different citation and reference styles. Plagiarism encompasses a wide spectrum of behaviors, from outright word-for-word copying of another's work to artful paraphrasing that re-states another author's idea without acknowledgment. We provide guidelines and resources to help students navigate the challenge of properly citing others' ideas and avoiding unethical uses of information.

Rationale

Research is the pursuit of knowledge and truth, so conducting research honestly is fundamental to the task. Every scholar has the responsibility to demonstrate absolute integrity in the reporting of data, in acknowledging the sources of ideas and information, and in providing thorough and correct documentation of those sources.

In this chapter we seek to shift some common perspectives on research integrity and the citation and documentation of sources. Many of our students have expressed a sense of fear or frustration about the topic of citations and bibliographies. They have too often been made to feel as if they could fail an assignment due to plagiarism for making an honest and fairly minor mistake in citation. On the other end of the spectrum we have had many students who assume that in a world of easy access to free information, there is no big deal in sharing and appropriating each other's work. Both attitudes are missing the mark and creating unnecessary problems for students, especially those involved in undergraduate research. Let us see if we can redefine the mark by clarifying a reasonable goal of honesty and integrity in scholarly work.

Plagiarism

The definition of plagiarism is taking someone else's ideas and representing them as your own. Plagiarism is a form of theft, as the ideas and hard work of one person are taken without their consent by someone else who hopes to benefit from them. In the U.S. and many other countries we share a legal standard and cultural understanding that each person's ideas (which are usually represented in the products of the ideas, such as works of art and pieces of writing) are uniquely their own. When the ideas are shared publicly—whether in the form of a film, blog post, song, essay, etc.—the creator/writer enters into an implicit trust with those who encounter it. The original creator/writer trusts that shared values and legal standards will keep their own name attached to it—that anyone else who shares or builds upon the work will give them the credit that is due.

Students and other scholars who incorporate others' ideas into their own are required to identify clearly the original sources of the ideas, no matter how easily accessible the information may be. Even those not intending to steal or cause harm may be committing ethics violations that have consequences, so it is incumbent on researchers to document the sources of information. When they intend to give credit but make an omission or other mistake students may be more guilty of sloppy scholarship than outright plagiarism. While it may not be an illegal offense, sloppy scholarship should be guarded against by taking care in the work and double-checking that all sources of information are correctly credited.

The intentional appropriation of others' ideas without giving credit is much more serious, of course. University policies and academic publishers dictate serious consequences for those who are caught plagiarizing or committing other violations in research ethics. Strict policies and severe consequences are intended to discourage such violations, for if plagiarism occurs without significant repercussions, everyone's work is diminished. For that reason, plagiarism can ruin a scholar's career. Other ethical and legal violations include fabricating or falsifying data and improperly treating human subjects/participants (including any violation of IRB guidelines).

Why There Are Different Citation and Documentation Styles

In our various academic disciplines we are all in agreement about the utmost importance of academic integrity and the lawful and ethical crediting of the sources of ideas. We have different guidelines for exactly how we do that crediting, though, based on our disciplinary epistemologies, or theories and ways of knowing (see Chapter 5). When students are required to use Modern Language Association (MLA) format in their first-year writing course and, just when they have that down, are expected to switch to the American Psychological Association (APA) style in their education or other social science classes—and then Chicago style in communication studies, they may be understandably frustrated. We have heard more than once students bemoaning different citation styles as a conspiracy to drive them mad.

Believe it or not, however, there are some sound reasons for the different expectations. We have found that understanding the epistemologies and underlying reasons for different citation and bibliographic styles helps ease the frustration. Graff and Birkenstein's (2014) *"They Say, I Say": The Moves that Matter in Academic Writing* very helpfully addresses the concept of templates in academic writing. Graff and Birkenstein point out that many of our disciplinary conventions follow certain patterns or templates, and that by learning some of the main ones we can master aspects of academic writing with more alacrity.

Our friend and colleague Herb Childress applies the idea of templates to understanding different citation systems and the disciplinary values they represent. Dr. Childress uses examples of MLA and APA parenthetical citations and bibliographic entries to make the point. MLA parenthetical citations require the author's last name and the page number on which the idea is stated. In APA format the parenthetical citation includes the author's last name and year of publication. The only time the page number is provided is when the text is quoted directly, which is rare in APA papers. Why the differences? MLA is the format used in the humanities, disciplines in which elegant writing and textual analysis are highly valued. Humanities scholars need the page number of an idea because reading the actual text, whether directly quoted or not, is important to them. APA, however, is used most often in social sciences, where different primary values are in play: timeliness—hence the use of the year of publication in the parenthetical citation—and the empirical/experimental findings themselves, as opposed to the prose in which they were reported. That is why APA papers include few if any direct quotations: the findings are what matter, not the way in which the researchers expressed them, so paraphrases do not lose the essence of the ideas.

The bibliographic entries of each style likewise reflect disciplinary priorities. On an MLA Works Cited page, authors' first and last names are listed, whereas APA uses last name only and initials. Why? The fullness of the human person is not only a subject of study but a deeply held value in the humanities. A scholar's full name conveys more about that person than his or her initials, including in many cases his or her gender identity. The scientific approach favored in disciplines that use APA style has a preference for more neutrality. There is no way to know the gender identity of a scholar from first and middle initials alone, and that is considered a good thing in objective research. Another notable difference between the two bibliographic styles is the placement of the year of publication: near the end of the entry in MLA Works Cited, but right after the authors' names—second thing in the entry—in APA References. The privileging of timely research is again the reason for the early placement of the date in APA References entries. In the humanities, however, timeliness may not matter at all. For people who study ancient and classical texts, there is timelessness in human wisdom. The year of publication is one of the least important pieces of information, so it is relegated to the end of the entry.

The OWL at Purdue

Even though we can understand some of the reasons for different citation and bibliographic styles, it is difficult to master and remember them. And even when we do master one or two styles with which we work most regularly, a new edition of the style book is published, and we have some new details to try to keep in mind. Fortunately holding all of that in one's own mind is not necessary beyond the basics, and keeping up with the changes can now be automatic. Thanks to the Online Writing Lab (OWL) at Purdue University, examples of citations and bibliographic entries for a wide variety of sources in several styles are readily and immediately available. We recommend bookmarking the website (https://owl.english.purdue. edu/owl/) and keeping it open while writing. Through a quick search and a look at some examples, anyone can be sure of correct, up-to-date citing and referencing.

Questions for Discussion

1 What "counts" as plagiarism?
2 What if you didn't mean to plagiarize?
3 What are the consequences for plagiarism in undergraduate research?
4 How can I identify typical mistakes in citing sources?

Reference

Graff, G. & Birkenstein, C. (2014). *"They say, I say": The Moves that Matter in Academic Writing*. New York: W. W. Norton.

8

DISSEMINATION OF RESULTS

The TV scientist who mutters sadly, "The experiment is a failure; we have failed to achieve what we had hoped for," is suffering mainly from a bad script writer. An experiment is never a failure solely because it fails to achieve predicted results. An experiment is a failure only when it also fails to adequately test the hypothesis in question, when the data it produces don't prove anything one way or another.
Robert M. Pirsig, *Zen and the Art of Motorcycle Maintenance*

Summary

Included in the CUR definition of undergraduate research is the phrase "contribution to the discipline." (Council on Undergraduate Research, n.d.) Like faculty scholarship, undergraduate research contributes to the discipline through dissemination of the work to other scholars, in the form of publications, conference presentations, performances, and exhibits. There is a growing number of opportunities for students to present, publish, and show their work, and this chapter provides a guide for students and faculty alike as to the various venues, conferences, symposia, and journals available to students.

Why Share Your Work?

The key attribute that transforms ordinary students doing research assignments into *scholars* is the dissemination of research results. Scholars are part of a *scholarly community* whose members learn from each other and advance the field of study. That learning from each other can only occur, of course, when scholars share their findings. One purpose of conducting research is to inform one's own thinking. But the more important reason to do research is to contribute to the discovery and creation of new knowledge. In sharing new knowledge, researchers further not only their own but also many others' understanding about the topic of study and contribute to the progression of the field.

Dissemination as a Defining Feature of Undergraduate Research

The definition of "undergraduate research" according to the national organization Council on Undergraduate Research (CUR) is "a faculty-mentored inquiry or investigation conducted by a student that *makes an original intellectual or creative contribution to the discipline*" (Council on Undergraduate Research, n.d.; emphasis added). The mentored inquiry or investigation would be incomplete without the *contribution* (through dissemination) to the discipline, or to another community as appropriate. That "original ... contribution to the discipline" is a very high standard; any scholar's work could shoot for that goal and not always get there, for any number of reasons. It could turn out that another scholar made the discovery first. Sometimes limitations of studies (see Chapter 5) are more significant than initially realized and then undermine the results. Or, even after a thoughtfully chosen design, a study may not go as planned, and the data could be inconclusive. Achieving publishable results that make a notable disciplinary contribution is not the only standard for successful undergraduate research, nor is it the only reason to disseminate findings. We usually talk with our students in terms of a slightly edited version of the CUR definition of undergraduate research: a faculty-mentored investigation that *seeks to make* an original intellectual or creative contribution. *Seeking to make* a contribution puts the focus on the process and purpose of conducting scholarly work. It does not depend on an entirely successful contribution. Having an orientation for your research efforts toward a community of disciplinary experts, peers, and/or practitioners (e.g., musicians, teachers, and therapists) makes your work more meaningful and scholarly than if you were gathering information solely for your own knowledge base.

We have found it even more useful to identify what makes undergraduate research a "high-impact practice" (Association of American Colleges and Universities, n.d.)—the characteristics or criteria of impactful scholarly experiences, rather than a one-size-fits-all definition. Osborn and Karukstis (2009) laid out four criteria of high-quality undergraduate research: mentorship by faculty; original work; acceptability in the discipline; and dissemination. In this chapter we are most interested in that last criterion, dissemination. Dissemination is considered a defining characteristic of undergraduate research because sharing the results of scholarly work with an audience of academics, peers, experts in the field, a community of practice (a group of people who share a common interest and wish to learn from each other about it), and/or the general public, completes the research process and is a powerful learning experience in its own right.

Engaging with an Authentic Audience

Have you ever wondered about the point of writing a research paper that only your instructor would ever read—and perhaps only cursorily, along with dozens of other students' assignments? We remember feeling let down at times during our student years, after investing late-night hours and some pretty good ideas in writing an essay, only to send it into the apparent void of a professor's paper pile. Our best professors wrote thoughtful responses to each student's work, and a couple of them even talked with us about it, but those were few and far between.

On the other hand, when students have the chance to engage with an authentic audience for their work beyond a single instructor they say they devote more time and effort to it. As university faculty we have witnessed the difference in the quality of student work when it will be disseminated in some way. The research and writing simply matter more when other people will read and respond to the product. As social creatures perhaps all of us are hard-wired to want to connect with others through our ideas and efforts. When others find our work thought-provoking, when they ask questions about it, and/or when they offer productive feedback, we tend to want to meet their expectations for good-quality work. For all of these reasons—the contributions that can be made to a scholarly community and field of study, the logical completion of the research process, and the higher level of effort and engagement inspired by addressing an audience—sharing the work is an essential aspect of undergraduate research.

What You Will Gain from Presenting and Publishing Your Scholarly Work

You may have heard the worrisome news of the last several years that the unemployment rate for recent college graduates in the U.S. is well above the national average—and is even above the unemployment rate for those over age 25 *without a college degree* (National Center for Education Statistics, 2016). Underemployment—which is defined as part-time employment for those who want to work full-time and/or employment in low-skilled jobs for people with college degrees—for college graduates under age 27 is even higher: over 40 percent in the U.S. Meanwhile, student-loan debt is at its highest point in history (National Center for Education Statistics, 2016). We share these statistics not at all to discourage you, but to make the case for doing everything you can during your undergraduate years to distinguish yourself in an intensely competitive job market and graduate-school environment.

The problem of the persistently high unemployment and underemployment rates for recent college graduates appears to be based at least in part in employers' beliefs that Millennials are unprepared for skilled work. A major survey of business and nonprofit leaders commissioned by the Association of American Colleges & Universities (AAC&U) found that employers see recent college graduates as ill-prepared for career success (Hart Research Associates, 2015). Employers gave low grades to recent college graduates on all of AAC&U's learning outcomes of a college education, including six skills deemed most important for career success across a range of nonprofit and for-profit industries: (1) oral communication; (2) working effectively on teams; (3) written communication; (4) ethical decision-making; (5) critical thinking and analysis; and (6) applying knowledge to real-world problems.

Oral Communication Skills

Implications of the research are that students who develop particularly valued skills are likely to stand out in a very tough employment environment. Nearly all business and nonprofit leaders surveyed said those six skills are more important than a job candidate's major or the university they attended (Hart Research Associates, 2015). In other words, students should be focused more on oral and written communication and critical, real-world problem-solving skills than worrying about the most marketable majors or the prominence of their university. All of the skills most valued by employers are developed exceptionally well through undergraduate research. And the top-ranked skill, oral communication, is principally cultivated through presenting scholarly work. Speaking articulately and confidently, and engaging interpersonally with a diversity of people are oral-communication skills that need extensive practice to develop.

It would not be at all surprising if you were reluctant (or even deathly afraid) to develop oral-communication skills by giving research presentations. Just about everyone experiences nervousness about public speaking, and for many the very idea brings on acute anxiety. According to the Chapman University Survey of American Fears, glossophobia—also known as stage fright or fear of public speaking—is one of the most common forms of personal anxiety (Chapman University, 2016). Fortunately there is a plethora of online and print resources to help manage anxiety about public speaking. More severe phobia can be eased through therapy, relaxation techniques, or hypnosis.

The best strategy of all for overcoming a fear of presenting is to practice over and over again, preferably in low-stakes settings. Take opportunities to present in less stressful situations, such as in a class with people you know and can trust to be on your side, or in a student research symposium on your campus, where dozens or even hundreds of your peers are going through the same experience along with you. Public speaking is truly something that gets easier by doing it. We recommend starting out with poster presentations, if feasible. Our students have found it much less nerve-racking to speak for a few minutes with one or two audience members at a time than to give a more formal talk. After even one poster presentation you will likely gain confidence in your ability to present your work and may feel more ready to try an oral presentation in a friendly environment. (Preparing poster and oral presentations is addressed later in this chapter.)

Written Communication Skills

The other critical career skill that is enhanced by sharing your research is written communication. Writing the content of an oral or poster presentation is an excellent means of developing drafting and revision skills. Writing about the results of research is especially suited to common workplace writing situations, such as reports and presentation materials. Showing a willingness to revise written work has been cited by employers as a rare and valuable trait. Your work to revise presentations—especially in consolidating a large amount of information into a succinct and effective poster or talk—can be noted in cover letters and interviews to your benefit.

Publishing your undergraduate research will take that distinction in written-communication skills to a whole new level. Composing a substantial paper that will be carefully read by an audience—as opposed to the quick grasp they would get from presentation slides or a poster—requires writing acumen and a longer process of drafting and revision. The work likely will pay off exceedingly well, though. Student papers published in Bridgewater State University's journal of undergraduate research, *The Undergraduate Review*, have been downloaded well *over a million times.* Students whose work appears in the journal, which is published in print as well as electronic form, report being asked about their research papers during interviews for internships, jobs, and graduate and professional school. They can include a link to their published paper in electronic applications, offering an at-the-ready writing sample that is not only well written, but also copyedited and nicely laid out by the journal editors. Since the published papers show up in online searches too, the students have discovered that when their names are Googled by potential employers or graduate admissions officers, what shows up, at or near the top of the results, is their published research. The benefits of that exposure of a student's best work are incalculable.

Where Can You Share Your Work?

The Rhetorical Situation

As you may have learned in an English composition course, the *audience, context,* and *purpose* of a piece of writing constitute its *rhetorical situation,* or the circumstances in which an argument is made. Like the concept of the rhetorical triangle explained in Chapter 5, the theory of the *rhetorical situation* derives from Aristotle's *Rhetoric,* an ancient Greek philosophical text about the art of effective speaking and writing. Bitzer (1968) adapted the concept for modern presenters and writers to explain how their claims are shaped by the intended audience (including readers), the context (or setting or framework in which the presenter/writer is working), and its purpose. The following examples of each aspect of the rhetorical situation—audience, context, and purpose—are intended to help illustrate its function. Imagine sharing your research in a venue mainly attended by your college or university's music professors. As experts in the field of study, the *audience* of music professors would expect high-level scholarly work. You might, for example, decide to include theoretical ideas with which only people who study music theory would be familiar. Alternatively, what if you were to present that same work in a talk at a multidisciplinary undergraduate conference attended by hundreds of college students majoring in a broad range of fields, many of whom have never taken a music course? In that presentation you would either omit some of the theory or include only a few key points with clear explanations. The audience determines a great deal of which content you share and how you present it.

The *context* (circumstance, setting, or framework) is the second determining factor. The presentation to the music faculty could occur in a departmental thesis defense, where you are expected to give a formal talk followed by challenging questions from the faculty. Your skill in answering the questions as well as your ability to present your most important results succinctly and clearly are being evaluated for a grade, and may even determine whether you graduate with honors. That high-stakes context would undoubtedly influence your selection of information and how you prepare for the questions. If, however, instead of justifying your work at a thesis defense you were presenting in a less intense situation, both the substance and style of your presentation would be different. Consider, for example, presenting a poster at your university's annual undergraduate-research symposium that is held on campus. Members of that same departmental music faculty might stop by your poster. Yet you would interact with them less formally, one or two at a time, rather than addressing the whole department at once. What you say to them would probably vary, based on how well you know each professor and how acquainted each is with your work. The context shapes the content, format, and design of the presentation.

The *purpose* of sharing the work also affects its substance and form. If you received an undergraduate-research grant from the department to support your work you would likely need to report to faculty on the selection committee about what you accomplished at the end of the grant period. Such a report could include major findings, challenges you encountered and how you addressed them, and a statement of gratitude for the opportunities afforded by the funding. But what if the grant were renewable and you wanted to request additional funds? You would still show what you accomplished with the first grant, but you would need to add a convincing explanation of how much further you would like to take the project and how a second round of funding would make that possible. In that grant-renewal request you would have a distinctly different purpose (asking for more money) and therefore would need to alter your report to achieve the hoped-for outcome. Each purpose has its own demands, and meeting those particular demands is essential to success.

This section is titled "Where Can You Share Your Work?" The answer to that question is contingent on the rhetorical situation, or the network of audience, context, and purpose. The main options are to publish your research in an academic journal and to present it at a conference, and there are multiple outlets and venues within those broad categories. The following possibilities for dissemination of undergraduate research in music begin with the most accessible opportunities and move roughly to the most selective.

Campus Symposium of Undergraduate Research

As the benefits of undergraduate research as a high-impact practice become ever more widely recognized, most four-year colleges and universities in the U.S. now offer opportunities for students to share their scholarly work in a campus symposium or showcase of undergraduate research, most often held at the end of the academic year. Some of those events feature poster presentations exclusively, while others include a mix of poster and oral presentations and, in some cases, art displays and music, dance, and theatre performances. The size and atmosphere of campus symposia vary a great deal too. On some campuses student-presenters are selected through a review process, whereas at other institutions everyone who wants to present is welcome, and many faculty even make a symposium presentation a course requirement, especially for capstones and other research-intensive courses. Awards for the highest quality research projects are given at many campus symposia.

Presenting in a campus symposium or showcase is an outstanding opportunity for several reasons. The symposium audience—other students, faculty and administrators, and some presenters' family members—offers a valuable and gratifying experience in addressing a real-world audience. Over the years we have each witnessed hundreds of students heading to their campus-symposium presentations with apprehension or dread, only to hear them say immediately afterward and, often, in the months and years that follow, that it was not nearly as intimidating as they had feared. Many of our students have even reported that the experience was fun. One of the most satisfying professional experiences for each of us is that first conversation with a student after a presentation. Students express relief that they overcame nervousness to give a solid presentation and, most exciting, gratitude for the experience of talking with people interested in their work. It has been through positive experiences at campus symposia that most of our students who have gone on to present at national conferences gained the confidence to do so.

We encourage you to present your work in whatever venue is available on your campus, whether a showcase of work from your department or school, or a university-wide event. The practice is invaluable, and each presentation is a legitimate point of distinction on your resume, especially with oral-communication skills so highly valued. If your college or university does not yet hold a symposium of student scholarship, you have a few options to pursue. The first is, with the support of faculty who know the quality of your work, you and some peers could request an opportunity in the department to share your work in panel presentations or posters. Many universities' larger events started with individual department efforts. And plenty of individual departments find that they value the small seminar-style symposia so much that they will keep hosting those events even if a larger showcase takes off on their campus. The second option is to locate an institution nearby that hosts an annual symposium of student work and ask whether students from neighboring campuses could participate. Our campus symposia welcome student-presenters from community colleges in the area. Finally, you may find a state or regional undergraduate-research conference with the welcoming environment of a campus-based event. The large Commonwealth of Massachusetts annual conference hosted by UMass-Amherst, for example, has a high rate of acceptance and inclusive feel.

National, State, and Regional Undergraduate-Research Conferences

Statewide and regional conferences of undergraduate research offer a moderate "step up" in presentation experience. Many such meetings accept most applicants, as they are not intended to be highly selective, but to give as many students as possible the opportunity to share their work beyond their home campuses.

The more selective state conferences are "posters at the capitol" events, for which a set number of students across that state are chosen to present posters, usually in the capitol building itself. The purposes of such events, beyond the great experience and prestige afforded to the student-presenters, are to show legislators and their staff members the importance and quality of research taking place in their districts and across the state, and, more or less directly, advocate for research and higher-education funding in the state. Traditionally, most of the posters at the capitol feature science, technology, engineering, and mathematics (STEM) research, but the rising recognition of the importance of scholarly work and funding for STEAM—STEM plus the arts—has brought more presentations from music and other arts disciplines.

As faculty and administrators with long-time participation in the National Conference on Undergraduate Research (NCUR) we cannot say enough about what a valuable experience that annual event offers for student-presenters.

NCUR has an over-30-year tradition of bringing together thousands of students from across the nation—as well as dozens from other countries—each year on a different college campus to present their research and creative scholarship. Over 3,500 students presented at the University of North Carolina—Asheville in April 2016, in the form of posters, oral presentations, art exhibits with gallery talks, and lecture-recitals (in which students in the performing arts perform a piece of music or dance and provide a brief lecture on it). NCUR has a high rate of acceptances, usually over 80 percent, and maintains strong quality in its presentations. Besides the distinction of presenting at a national conference with a large, engaged audience, NCUR offers the opportunity to meet students in your own field and every major imaginable from across the country and the world. The conference hosts a graduate-school fair of hundreds of different programs, inspiring keynote speakers, and social events. Inexpensive excursions in the local area are often available on the Saturday the conference ends, as well.

Disciplinary Academic Meetings/Conferences

As the tide of undergraduate research has swept through higher education in the last two decades, many of the disciplinary professional organizations in which university faculty participate and present their scholarly work have provided venues for undergraduates in their respective areas to present too. Our universities' undergraduate-research offices regularly receive notifications of new opportunities for students to present at academic organizations' regional and national meetings. Most of those organizations have carved out a session for undergraduates within the larger meeting, giving students the dual benefit of attending presentations by scholars in their field of study while having a space for presenting at an undergraduate level. Putting undergraduates side by side with renowned scholars can be intimidating for the students. Nonetheless, a few disciplinary conferences have gone that route, successfully bringing together undergraduates, graduate students, and professors in shared sessions.

Opportunities in music include the College Music Society, which hosts regional and national conferences that welcome student participation. Every state has an annual conference for music educators, and there is usually a conference strand specifically for undergraduates who plan to become music teachers. Some of the presentation opportunities in music include composition competitions and performance showcases. The National Association for Music Education offers opportunities for student composers and future music teachers to share their work as well to compete for cash prizes. See Chapter 15 for an example of student composers who performed their work at a regional electronic music festival.

Undergraduate Research Journals

Undergraduate students who get their work published are most often published in a journal of student work. Many colleges and universities publish their own students' scholarship in a campus-based journal, in electronic and/or print format. In addition to campus-based journals, a few college and university consortia (associations of several institutions joined by region or mission), such as the Council of Public Liberal Arts Colleges, and state-university systems publish journals featuring work by students at any of the member institutions.

A few student journals publish work by undergraduates in multiple disciplines from any college or university. They include the *Journal of Student Research* (www.jofsr.com/index.php/path/index), *American Journal of Undergraduate Research* (www.ajuronline.org/), and *Journal of Undergraduate Research and Scholarly Excellence* (http://jur.colostate.edu/).

Peer-Reviewed Academic Journals

If your audience is made up of professionals in the field and your purpose is to demonstrate high-level competence as a scholar—perhaps with the goal of attending a selective graduate program in an area of music—publishing your work in a peer-reviewed journal may be your goal (see Chapter 2 for an explanation of the peer-review process). In that case your research would have to be not just mentored by a professor but actually a professional collaboration between your faculty mentor and yourself. Publishing in a peer-reviewed journal is the "gold standard," or most prestigious level, of dissemination of scholarly work. Undergraduate research is not usually considered for such publications unless the work is coauthored with a faculty member, as meeting the standards for such journals usually require expertise in the field that most scholars attain through graduate study and in their academic careers. If you are collaborating with a professor on a shared project, your professor may already be thinking in terms of a peer-reviewed publication. Having papers accepted for such journals is an expectation for university faculty as they seek tenure and promotion; plus most academics enjoy disseminating their work as part of their engagement in the field of study. If a peer-reviewed journal publication is the goal, your professor will likely take the lead as first author, but the expectations for your contributions will likely be demanding. Experts in the field of study are the arbiters of the quality of the research and writing.

Forms of Dissemination

Abstract

In order to present your scholarly work you will first need to submit an *abstract*, or summary, of the work. Acceptance to present at a conference is based on the quality of the abstract. (Sometimes, though rarely, additional documents such as a personal statement are requested.) If you are accepted to present, your abstract will appear in the conference program.

An abstract is a one-paragraph overview of a project or study. An abstract for a conference may need to be as brief as 60 words or may go as long as 350 words (for NCUR); check the conference's "call for abstracts" for requirements.

Write the abstract after your work is complete, or is at least far enough along that you have initial findings to report. The abstract focuses on results and the significance of the work. It is written in past tense for most disciplines, but can be in the present tense for music projects. The abstract for a conference presentation should not be written in future tense. (In other words, you should not submit the same abstract if you created one before you began your work, for a research proposal.)

At the top of the page include a thoughtful, interesting, and informative title, with the first letter of each main word capitalized. Only use quotation marks or italics if your title includes the title of a published or a quoted phrase. Be sure to include the name(s) of the author(s). An abstract is usually structured with the following parts:

- Sentences 1–2 (or more on a longer abstract): Context/background/need. What is the problem, question, need, or important context that prompted your work?
- The next 2–3 sentences: The purpose/focus of the study or project (you can state the purpose explicitly, e.g., "The purpose of this research was to determine … to examine … to analyze … to learn … to investigate … to assess … to research … to create … to compose …").
- The next 2–3 sentences: statement of the methods or process you undertook in order to fulfill the purpose.
- The rest of the abstract (2–5 sentences): explanation of the results of your work (what you discovered or created) and its significance/implications. Consider how your project relates to others' published work. How will other scholars or the discipline overall benefit from your results? If applicable, how could you or other scholars take your study further?

Posters

Academic posters constitute a distinct genre that calls for planning and presentation of ideas in ways very different from research essays. A poster should not be designed as a shortened research paper with images added. Like any other text—in any genre or rhetorical situation—posters should be designed with the audience, context, and purpose in mind.

Poster presentations offer certain advantages over traditional modes of presenting music scholarship. For one, many more presenters and audience members can be accommodated during a single session, as opposed to the panels of just three or four presenters at a time that are typical in oral-presentation sessions and lecture-recitals. So as participation in undergraduate research grows at most institutions, accommodating hundreds of presenters at campus symposia and other conferences will be more feasible with at least some of the arts and humanities students (not just those in the sciences) presenting posters. Another asset of poster presenting is that students are required to think about their work in new ways, including how to articulate it more succinctly and in a different format. Poster presenters not only gain skills in consolidating points into the content of the poster, but also in their "poster talk" or "elevator speech"—the two–three-minute synopsis of the study they need to have ready to deliver. Preparing posters also helps students develop skills of visual rhetoric and design thinking, as they consider how to represent their points in visually appealing configurations.

The rhetorical situation (audience, context, and purpose) of poster presentations prompt additional considerations. Because of the opportunities for rich one-on-one interactions with audience members, poster presenters should ensure that the research question, purpose of the study, and major findings are immediately clear. If audience members can grasp the main points right away, the interactions can lead to more nuanced discussion. Consider what an engaged audience member needs to understand quickly in order to ask informed questions during the session. At the same time, think about what a casual observer should walk away with after a more brief perusal of the poster. The uniqueness or distinctiveness of the work should be evident.

Research posters usually include the following parts:

- Summary/abstract or 2–3-sentence thesis.
- Brief introductory/contextual info, including the research question(s).
- Theory or critical approach of the researcher.
- Explanation of the process or methods.
- Findings/results/main argument.
- Significance of the work.
- Key quotations from primary texts, participants, and/or the research paper, if applicable.
- Photos, maps, illustrations, graphs (making up at least one-third of the poster).
- Bibliography, if brief (long bibliographies can be made available as handouts and/or as shared cloud documents).

The poster document is usually created as a single PowerPoint slide, set up with the dimensions of the poster. A typical size is 42 inches in width by 36–38 inches in height, though some conferences have smaller boards available and will therefore require smaller posters. The following suggestions are for the structure and design of the poster:

- At the top, include the title, presenter's name, mentor's name, and your university's and/or sponsoring organization's name and logo.
- Below that heading of the title and names, set up three or four equal-sized columns for text and images.
- The text for most of the poster should be in 32–70-point type so that it is readable at a distance of a few feet. The title can be larger (80–100-point), and captions for images can be smaller (22–24-point).
- Use a white or light background; it makes the poster easier to read, and keeping a white background costs less to print because less ink is used.
- Use dark, coordinating colors for the body of the text, headings, borders and lines, etc.
- Align the columns and use text boxes and borders to create neat lines and a sense of order. Avoid "jagged edges" by placing borders around some text boxes and fully justifying text, i.e., aligning it with both margins.
- Follow a logical sequence and structure for reading left to right and top to bottom.
- Maintain consistency in fonts, styles, sizes of text, and width of text boxes.
- Keep some "white space" for ease of reading and visual calm.
- Break up large amounts of text with images that you have permission to use and that are cited. Text should take up less than two-thirds of the poster.
- Make sure that photos and logos are of high resolution. They should not appear pixilated when viewing the poster at 100% zoom.
- Proofread meticulously before sending the document to the printer, and, if possible, ask at least one other person to proofread it too. Minor errors are easy to miss on a computer screen but show up large on a poster.

In addition to these guidelines, we recommend "Poster-making 101" by Brian Pfohl at Bates College, available online at http://abacus.bates.edu/~bpfohl/posters/#essentials

Oral Presentations

Oral presentations include several of the elements of posters. See the bullet points listed earlier under "Research posters usually include the following parts." The images and bibliography can be presented in slides, which accompany most oral presentations. Although the basic elements of research presentations are present no matter the format, differences in genre between posters and talks require distinct considerations. An oral presentation requires a more formal, planned out, scripted (to some extent) presentation *in the moment.* The content of a poster is mostly fixed, so the live presenting is short and less formal—a few minutes at most with each member of the audience. Oral presenters, however, have a longer time with the audience (usually 12–15 minutes, plus a few minutes for answering audience questions) that is fixed and often strictly enforced; staying focused and organized is essential to completing the presentation in the scheduled session.

Presenters of talks cultivate highly valued skills of public speaking that include effective use of body language, eye contact, and voice projection in addition to the writing and rhetorical skills developed by working on the content. Our best advice for preparing oral presentations is first to think about the engaging presentations you have attended, as well as those that were unsuccessful in maintaining your interest. What have other presenters done to maintain your attention or to turn you off from their presentation? How have you seen slides and other visual aids used effectively and ineffectively during oral presentations? We find with our students that it is easy to identify what has gone poorly in ineffective presentations—everything from the speaker reading straight from notes without making adequate eye contact with the audience, to reading straight from the slides, back facing the audience; from low voice volume to verbal tics and other nervous habits; from misspellings and typos on slides to mispronunciation of important terms. Simply avoiding those goes a long way toward giving a good presentation.

As you prepare your script and slides, consider what a non-expert could reasonably retain without losing interest, while also ensuring that you engage knowledgeable audience members. That balance usually requires briefly defining some key terms and theories before moving straight to the results and significance of your work.

In addition to writing the script and designing slides, oral presenters should prepare for audience questions. Work with your faculty mentor and classmates to brainstorm what kinds of questions you should anticipate and how you will answer them. It is just as helpful to prepare what to say when you do not know the answer to an audience question. There is no shame in acknowledging the limits of your study or explaining that the scope of your work did not encompass what is being asked. If you are prepared for responding you will be far less anxious about difficult questions.

Lecture-Recitals

Lecture-recitals are a unique form of presenting scholarship in the performing arts. They include the components and format of an oral presentation, with a performance piece added. A lecture-recital by Alexander Heinrich at NCUR in 2012 stood out as an exemplar. Titled "Ginastera: Putting Argentina on the Map of Western Classical Music," Alex Heinrich's lecture-recital began with an explanation of the three compositional periods of Alberto Ginastera (1916–

1983) and then explored how his Argentinian and broader South American cultures influenced Ginastera, who altered traditional musical elements while also paying homage to his country's musical heritage. The lecture was broken up by Alex alternately taking a seat at the piano to play excerpts of Ginastera's compositions. The audience heard *about* and then heard *examples of* Ginastera's stylistic development across three compositional periods.

Journal Articles

In order to prepare a manuscript of your undergraduate research for possible publication in any type of journal, including an undergraduate-research journal, we recommend the following considerations.

The first step is to determine early on that publication is your goal so that you orient yourself from the beginning to do work that could be publishable. Writing a publishable paper starts well in advance of the actual writing. Thinking about whether you want to publish your work at the beginning of your research, when you are focusing the topic and research question, is not too soon. That early goal can help you set up a study that takes on something new, interesting, timely, and significant enough to interest journal editors, reviewers, and readers.

You would also need to decide early on what type of paper to write. Full articles of 15–30 pages are the most rigorous and thorough academic papers. They are completed reports of scholarship of importance in the field. Research briefs are much shorter pieces (typically 2–8 pages) that summarize the research and highlight the most important findings and implications. Practice-based papers of varying length include scholarly research but focus on community-based or other practitioner work, with implications for people doing work in schools, therapeutic settings, and other places in the community.

Various journals—including student publications, popular or opinion magazines, trade journals (dedicated to a particular industry), and campus or regional-interest periodicals, as well as peer-reviewed/scholarly journals—publish certain types of papers and often have particular page-length requirements. Choosing the target journal—the right journal for your work—is therefore important in the early stages as well. It can be difficult to select the right journal unless you are aiming for a campus undergraduate-research journal, so plan to spend some time researching the best option to submit to first. Do not submit your work to more than one journal at the same time. In order to determine whether a journal is the right one for your work is to look at the articles it has recently published. Is yours at a similar level of work and within the scope of what the journal publishes?

Keep in mind the criteria that the reviewers will be using to evaluate your paper. The journal guidelines may include evaluation criteria. If not, questions such as these are fairly typical for academic journals:

- Does the paper contain new and interesting material?
- Are points presented concisely and in a well-organized format?
- Are the methods explained in a way that they can be replicated?
- Are the findings/results presented clearly and convincingly?
- Is the analysis/discussion relevant and insightful?
- Are the implications/conclusions supported by the evidence presented?
- Are the vocabulary, style, and tone at a high level of sophistication?
- Are any figures, tables, and images necessary and well designed?
- Are all sources cited in the text and included in the bibliography?

Pay close attention to the journal's submission guidelines. They generally include detailed expectations for the format of papers, submission procedures, and copyright policies. Most journal editors will not waste time on manuscripts that do not align with the guidelines.

Questions for Discussion

1 What are you most apprehensive about prior to presenting?
2 How can you put your best foot forward?
3 What do you feel you will gain from the experience?

References

Association of American Colleges and Universities. (n.d.). High-impact practices. Retrieved from www.aacu.org/resources/high-impact-practices (accessed 14 April 2017).
Bitzer, L. F. (1968). The rhetorical situation. *Philosophy and Rhetoric*, 1, 1–14.
Chapman University. (2016). Survey of American fears. Retrieved from www.chapman.edu/fearsurvey (accessed 14 April 2017).
Council on Undergraduate Research. (n.d.). What is the definition of undergraduate research? Retrieved from www.cur.org/about_cur/frequently_asked_questions_/#2 (accessed 14 April 2017).
Hart Research Associates. (2015). *Falling Short? College Learning and Career Success*. Retrieved from www.aacu.org/sites/default/files/files/LEAP/2015employerstudentsurvey.pdf
National Center for Education Statistics. (2016). Employment rates of college graduates. Retrieved from https://nces.ed.gov/fastfacts/display.asp?id=561
Osborn, J. & Karukstis, K. (2009). The benefits of undergraduate research, scholarship, and creative activity. In M. K. Boyd & J. L. Wesemann (eds), *Broadening Participation in Undergraduate Research: Fostering Excellence and Enhancing the Impact*. (pp. 41–53). Washington, DC: Council on Undergraduate Research.

9

MUSIC PERFORMANCE AND RELATED TOPICS

Don't only practice your art, but force your way into its secrets; art deserves that, for it and knowledge can raise man to the Divine.
Ludwig van Beethoven, letter to Emilie, quoted in *Musical News*, 1812

Music films are great, but they can never compete with a live performance. Live music is what it is. It's the whole point. You experience it in the moment.
Jonathan Demme

In terms of brain development, musical performance is every bit as important educationally as reading and writing.
Oliver Sacks, "Six Questions for Oliver Sacks," *Harper's Magazine*

Summary

This chapter explores various facets of musical performance including the process of conducting meaningful background research, preparing and writing effective program notes, and other original contributions within the discipline. Projects in this area help students make the case that they are performing artists and not just craftspeople learning a trade, and that creative contributions through performance can be as valuable as peer-reviewed publications in other disciplines. Sample program notes, possible topics, and representative undergraduate research abstracts in the realm of music performance are included to act as a springboard for creative inquiry by undergraduate music majors and others. Sample abstracts from conferences and questions for discussion follow.

Introduction

Goals of an undergraduate capstone experience often aim to:

- engage students in advanced disciplinary or interdisciplinary work to synthesize and culminate the students' learning;
- have students produce a final paper, report, creative work, portfolio, exhibition, performance, or other document or presentation appropriate for the discipline;
- require students to share their work with an audience as determined by their respective department.

The scholarly element of a capstone in music performance often takes the form of a recital with program notes. Background research can provide deep insights into the composer's intentions and an understanding of the wider context of the music that may radically affect a student's musical interpretation. To write effectively about their findings, students must conduct meaningful research into the music that is to be performed. What does the process of researching a musical work look like?

Process

This section borrows heavily from Nigel Scaife's "Writing Programme Notes: A Guide for Diploma Candidates." It has been paraphrased and distilled to its most salient elements pertaining to undergraduate research in music performance. Naturally, understanding the different components of the piece is the first step. While practicing the piece from the outset, pay attention to the harmonies, melodies, structure, and style, but also think about it in a wider musical and historical context through separate study. The theoretical foundation of a composition may enhance the performer's ability to effectively convey the composer's intentions, both in performance and in a written manner, even if they are not included in the program notes. Historical performances practices of the day may also provide a critical perspective; in fact the work might have been composed for a different instrument, or an earlier version of the instrument upon which you will perform. A description of the original instrument and the conventions that relate to the style of performance on that instrument may enhance the experience for the audience. An excellent starting point for researching musical performance practice is *The Historical Performance of Music* by Colin Lawson and Robin Stowell (1999).

Listening to other works by the composer whose music is to be performed can be very useful in getting ready to perform. Also listen to similar works of that genre. A valuable endeavor in preparing a Chopin nocturne would be to play through and listen to other nocturnes, not only by Chopin but also by other composers of the time. John Field, for example, cultivated the nocturne both as an idea and a genre, and associated it inescapably with the piano. This kind of study reveals what the nocturne you are preparing has in common with others and what elements make it unique, thereby aiding in stylistic understanding and interpretation. You may also consider differences between Mozart's piano and the modern instrument and how this may affect techniques such as pedaling in performance; or what previous music influenced Chopin's flowery melodic writing. All this provides historical context to properly inform authentic performances.

Primary and secondary sources are both useful and it is important to understand the distinction between them (see Chapter 5 of this book). Primary sources are documents such as manuscripts and letters that provide first-hand testimony or information about a specific work, while secondary sources include other documents such as biographies, dictionaries, and histories that provide indirect context or commentary on the work. General music history textbooks such as Grout and Palisca's *A History of Western Music* offer an excellent starting point for research by providing an overview of a musical period or composer. *The New Grove Dictionary of Music and Musicians* has detailed information and the entries often include bibliographies that cite further sources on specific works and composers. Depending on which edition of the music is used for performance, there may be valuable written information about the piece, preceding or subsequent to the notes.

Especially given all the information and the lack of accountability on the Internet, be critical of all sources. Websites such as Wikipedia may be a good place to start for research, but try to find where the information came from originally; one of the most valuable sections might be the bibliography. Writing a worthy set of program notes involves reaching conclusions from the information gathered. The notes should reflect your own experience of the music.

Preparing Program Notes

Program notes provide audience members with details that inform their hearing and enhance their understanding of the music being performed. Audiences will find focused, detailed information about a couple of aspects of the music more valuable than a jumbled amalgam of facts about the work or composer. For this reason, effective program notes emphasize material that is directly related to the performance and avoid information that is tangential, as they are too brief to address every aspect of a work.

For each piece in a program, an entry might address:

- how the piece came to be written;
- the history of the work's reception;
- the relationship between the work and biographical details of the composer's life;

- the place of the composition within the composer's *oeuvre*;
- the musical form of the work;
- the compositional genre that the piece represents;
- compositional techniques employed in the work;
- relevant information about the poet or the poetry (for vocal music);
- the relationship between music and the text (for vocal music);
- a discussion of the piece's programmatic elements (for programmatic works);
- the significance of the composition in the performing repertoire.

Inappropriate topics and things to avoid include:

- general information about the composer's biography not directly relevant to the piece;
- the performer's personal feelings about the piece;
- technical challenges experienced by the performer while preparing the piece;
- over-emoting;
- overly technical terminology;
- musical examples;
- blow-by-blow musical descriptions.

Each program note should include the title and composer of the work in the same format as printed in the program. Music style guides such as Holoman's *Writing About Music: A Style Sheet* describe how to format titles of different genres. In addition to some of the topics listed above, a well selected quotation from the composer, a noted scholar, or highly regarded performer can boost the credibility of program notes. Quotes should be limited in length, so as not to detract from original words and ideas. The author or speaker of any quote used in a program note should be identified.

Other Performance Research and Original Contributions

Other ways of making an original contribution to the discipline of music performance include performing a work for the first time, or recording a piece that is out of print or has not been previously recorded. This includes new arrangements, performed or recorded for the first time. This could, of course, be combined with program notes for a complete package. Many other suggestions for projects are listed below. Advancing the discipline in these ways allows an undergraduate researcher to contribute in ways that a faculty member might contribute in their own research endeavors.

SAMPLE PROGRAM NOTE (BY MSU STUDENT ANDREW MAJOR)

Piano Sonata No. 8 in C minor
("Pathétique") Op. 13

Ludwig van Beethoven
(1770–1827)

Grave; Allegro di molto e con brio

It was, quite unusually, Beethoven himself who coined the famous nickname of this sonata. He called it "Grande sonate pathétique" when it was published in Vienna at the end of 1799. Beethoven understood the word "pathétique" to mean intense or emotional, and those qualities saturate this sonata, often in quite different ways. Beethoven's choice of key for this piece is essential: C minor was the key he turned to for his darkest and most dramatic music and it would later be the key of his Fifth Symphony, Coriolan Overture, and the Funeral March of "Eroica." By the time of this sonata's composition, Beethoven had already composed a piano trio, a piano sonata, a string trio, and a string quartet in C minor, but none of these works approach the austere power of the "Pathétique," the earliest great manifestation of his so-called "C-minor mood."

Beyond its raw emotional power, this sonata is notable for its experiments with form. The piece opens with a slow introduction (his first in a piano sonata) marked *Grave*, an indication of solemnity as well as slow speed. The powerful chords lead to a sudden plummet down a chromatic run into the main body of the movement marked *Allegro di molto e con brio*. The materials here are simple: the opening theme is essentially a run up the C-minor scale set at a quiet dynamic, but these simple elements are infused with vast power, and soon the music is rushing forward with furious energy. The second theme, fleet and singing, is decorated with mordents (short trills). At the point the development should begin, the music comes to an abrupt stop, and the dark imposing chords of the *Grave* introduction return. Only then does Beethoven allow the development to proceed, climaxed by remarkable harmonic progressions, until Beethoven brings back a reminiscence of the *Grave* before the brief coda hurls the movement to its close.

The "Pathétique" is one of Beethoven's most popular works, and this was true even in his own time. The pianist Ignaz Moscheles, at age 10, left an astonishing account of the sonata's effect on young musicians of the era:

It was about this time that I learnt from some school-fellows that a young composer had appeared at Vienna, who wrote the oddest stuff possible—such as no one could either play or understand; crazy music, in opposition to all rule; and that this composer's name was Beethoven. On returning to the library to satisfy my curiosity as to this so-called genius, I found there Beethoven's Sonata pathétique. This was in the year 1804. My pocket-money would not suffice for the purchase of it, so I secretly copied it. The novelty of its style was so attractive to me, and I became so enthusiastic in my admiration of it, that I forgot myself so far as to mention my new acquisition to my master, who reminded me of his injunction, and warned me not to play or study any eccentric production until I had based my style upon more solid models. Without, however, minding his injunctions, I seized upon the pianoforte works of Beethoven as they successively appeared, and in them found a solace and a delight such as no other composer afforded me.

Other Suggested Research Topics in Music Performance

- Create new perspectives on performance such as incorporating multi-media power-point song recitals, or other novel performance approaches;
- research new evidence about the technique of an instrument;
- find effective mindfulness-based practicing techniques;
- incorporate new technologies into performance;
- investigate or use historical performance practices such as the use of a bassett clarinet to perform Mozart's Clarinet Concerto in A major, K622; or a baroque bow to perform baroque compositions on instruments with gut strings;
- commission and/or perform new or recently discovered works;
- study the effect music performance has on motivation;
- examine the results of certain types of practice methods on performance;
- survey musicians about performance anxieties and possible remedies;
- analyze the ways music performance majors are using entrepreneurship to create new opportunities in performance;
- examine the effectiveness of collage concerts from audience and performers' perspectives;
- do qualitative research on ensemble participation as a retention tool;
- study the flash mob performance phenomenon and its history;
- study indigenous music and its impact in your region of the world.

Sample Abstracts Submitted to NCUR

www.cur.org/conferences_and_events/student_events/ncur/archive/

The Effect of Using the Alexander Technique for Improved Music Performance

Michael Sharp, presenter; Reeves Shulstad, mentor; Hayes School of Music, Appalachian State University, Boone, NC, 2011

The Alexander Technique, a method that retrains the body to move more effectively developed by F. M. Alexander (1869–1955), can be useful in improving a musician's performance as well as their everyday living. Human beings can develop bad habits that cause unnecessary tension and pain throughout their bodies; we are all prone to blame that pain on an external source instead of asking ourselves if we are using ourselves correctly. Using the knowledge of how to properly use our bodies and self through the Alexander Technique can allow performers to stop feeling tension and realize that they use too much effort to perform a certain action. For musicians, when using the Alexander Technique nervousness no longer becomes an issue, the music becomes more beautiful and sounds more effortless, and the musician has more fun performing. Based on surveys and interviews of the students and faculty that are involved in the Alexander Technique classes in the School of Music at Appalachian State University, this project will reveal how using the Alexander Technique impacts nervousness, the quality of sound, and the musician's enjoyment of the performance.

This Is My Tuba: An Interactive Multi-Media Performance

Brett Copeland, author; John Fritch, mentor; College of Humanities, Arts & Sciences, University of Northern Iowa, Cedar Falls, IA, 2014

In this work, I am putting to use the different skills and means of expression I have learned. My goal is to combine all aspects of my undergraduate studies into a single composition that is both aurally and visually captivating. I have created a composition for tuba with interactive electronics and video based on Jean Sibelius' symphonic poem "Finlandia." This work is approximately 8 minutes in length. This work is composed in the style of theme and variations with the theme from Sibelius' "Finlandia." Sibelius' piece was composed for the Press Celebrations held in Helsinki in 1899, where the Finnish people protested the increasing censorship by Russia. "Finlandia" was the last movement of a seven movement work that aimed to reflect Finnish history. The piece was received as a great success by the Finnish people and was re-published as a stand-alone work. "Finlandia" was so popular it became the unofficial national hymn of Finland. Russians sought to censor the piece, as it was a work of protest, but the title was changed many times and the theme was disguised to avoid being censored. One of the more flippant alternate titles used was "Happy Feelings at the Awakening of the Finnish Spring." The historical context of this piece contributes to the fact that it is such a powerful and inspirational work. I aim to use the historical context to fuel my performance and allow the nature and integrity of the piece show. The theme and variations are based on the different masquerades that were employed with the original work. This will be apparent not only in the musical sense regarding form and notation but also in an emotional and historical sense as seen in the video. To achieve this, I will use a multitude of different video effects to respond to the different sonic atmospheres being created. This piece features live performance on tuba manipulated by the software packages Ableton Live and MAX/MSP to produce the electronic sound and video portions. Live sounds are processed through the computer and combined with pre-recorded samples to produce a truly unique soundscape that would be impossible to replicate by either purely electronic or purely acoustic music. The video portion began its life as a series of naturalistic photographs of Finland and Russian landscapes. The photos were then edited and put together using video effects housed in MAX/MSP software. The video will be manipulated by MAX/MSP to produce a performance that is both aurally and visually spectacular for the audience.

A Rose by Any Name: Are All Editions of Music Created Equally?

Chris Bosch, author; Deborah Nemko; Bridgewater State University, Bridgewater, MA, 2014

Does it matter what edition of music we play from? Do small details in a publication matter to the performer or listener? Through the performance of excerpts from several versions of Fryderyk Chopin's Nocturne in F minor Op. 55 No. 1 including Schirmer Publications, the C.F. Peters Edition, and the National Edition of the Works of Fryderyk Chopin, and a free-download from the internet, I will demonstrate to the listener that small differences in publications make a great impact on the performance. In Chopin's music particularly, these editions tend to contain more differences, and therefore there is a large difference in the quality of editions. This is due to the fact that in Chopin's music, many of the phrases are meant to sound improvisatory, due to the fact that Chopin himself was a good improviser and used it in many of his performances. This presentation will give musicians an understanding of what makes certain editions better than others and can offer some insight to non-musicians what musicians consider when performing a piece, and the events and thought processes that go into learning a piece of music. The presentation will conclude with a performance of Nocturne in F minor, which will demonstrate the points made in the presentation.

Conclusion

Although some performers might think that what they do is not research, music performance is a legitimate academic field, with tenured professors at research universities mentoring students through bachelors, masters, and doctoral degrees, so it stands to reason that undergraduate researchers can participate fully in it. There are many aspects to performance, and undergraduate research projects can cover the gamut, from a comprehensive approach in preparing a senior recital to the many other contributions outlined earlier. Certainly projects of significant quality and depth serve to legitimize not only the projects themselves but the whole field of music performance as a discipline worthy of research.

Questions for Discussion

1 When is performance really not research?
2 Why do some performers succeed with a very small research component?
3 Should all senior recitals have a research component? What might this look like?
4 What are ways to make original contributions to the field of music through performance?
5 Does research need to be presented at senior recitals or should it just be done "behind the scenes" beforehand?
6 What are the benefits of thoroughly researching a piece being performed?

References

Bean, J. & Myerson, J. (2000). *Margaret Fuller, Critic: Writings from the* New-York Tribune, *1844–1846*. New York: Columbia University Press. Retrieved from https://books. google.com/books?id=WnuDCgAAQBAJ&pg=PA74&lpg=PA74&dq
Grout, D. J. & Palisca, C. V. (2001). *A History of Western Music* (6th edn). New York: Norton.
Holoman, D. K. (2008). *Writing About Music: A Style Sheet*. Berkeley, CA: University of California Press.
Lawson, C. & Stowell, R. (1999). *The Historical Performance of Music*. Cambridge: Cambridge University Press.
Sadie, S. & Tyrrell, J. (2001). *The New Grove Dictionary of Music and Musicians*. Oxford: Grove.
Scaife, N. (2005). *Writing Programme Notes: A Guide for Diploma Candidates*. London: Associated Board of the Royal Schools of Music. Retrieved from www.abrsm.org/ resources/writingProgNotesApr05.pdf (accessed 2 October 2016).

10

IS MUSIC COMPOSITION
ORIGINAL RESEARCH?

If a composer could say what he had to say in words he would not bother trying to say it in music.

Gustav Mahler, letter to Max Marschalk, 1896

I have learned throughout my life as a composer chiefly through my mistakes and pursuits of false assumptions, not by my exposure to founts of wisdom and knowledge.

Igor Stravinsky

Summary

Achievement levels in composition vary greatly, from college freshmen writing original melodies for the first time, to the great symphonies that Mozart wrote at a similar age. And how is it usually done? Has the process changed with the advent of computer music notation? This chapter will explore the criteria for evaluating the strength of a compositional research project, what background research needs to be undertaken and documented, and how such work might be seen and heard by a variety of audiences from experts to the average listener. Quotes from student composers will be followed by sample project abstracts.

Introduction

Using computer music notation programs such as Sibelius or Finale, even an engineering major with no musical background could, with a little guidance, compose a string quartet. The software shows a different color when the instruments are out of range, and this can be easily corrected. Some listeners, upon hearing a rendition of this quartet, either played on the computer or by live musicians, would not be able to tell the difference between a bona fide modern string quartet and this example of non-composition. But this could not be classified as research. Moving up on the spectrum toward real undergraduate research in music composition, college music majors could compose string quartets in similar ways, with the addition of conscious decisions as to what might work well musically. In most cases however, without serious thought and background training with respect to form, harmony, counterpoint, linear aesthetics, and analysis of existing compositions, these would still be hard to classify as undergraduate research projects. Although the latter example is certainly creative, and in exceptional cases could be great original music, a little more thorough study is generally required to make sure the process is well understood and can be communicated successfully to a wider audience.

What Is the Process?

Musical composition often starts with an inspiration. However, students are advised not to just wait for an inspiration, but to understand that daily discipline applies to composing, just as it does to practicing. Inspiration can come from a wide variety of sources, including nature, emotions, visual art, pre-existing music, specific combinations of instruments, or a particular playing style. Background training in harmony, counterpoint, form, orchestration, and music history allow the student composer to draw upon the skills necessary to innovate. Planning a composition often involves thinking about the big picture, as an architect would, and sketching out the form before delving into the details at the micro level. For example, if one looks at Beethoven's symphony sketches in the British Museum, it is clear that although he had certain melodic fragments in mind, and wrote them down, he left large blank spaces so he could plan out his intentions for the musical direction on a large scale and fill in the detail later.

Often the composer will have to do some research into the types of compositional techniques needed to achieve a certain effect, whether they be melodic, harmonic, rhythmic, contrapuntal, or formal. Many composers have drawn upon influences for their compositions from travels to foreign countries for example, and in those cases they often did extensive research on the particular sounds they heard, to authentically replicate the styles. This could also involve historical research into techniques used by previous composers. Score analysis is a time-intensive process and can yield results similar to reading a scientific study. By recognizing and imitating patterns used in effective compositions, students can learn skills that do not come from simply studying music theory.

Whether one uses computer music notation or begins sketching with a pencil and manuscript paper, it takes patience and diligence to move from the sketch to the first complete draft. There is usually a long period of trial and error before the composer is happy with the finished product. It is common knowledge that Johannes Brahms worked on his first symphony off and on for 15 years, perhaps intimidated by the triumphant Symphony No. 9 that Beethoven composed in the 1820s. Following the final draft there is usually a fair amount of editing, to make sure the dynamics, phrasing, articulation marks, etc. are entered accurately and that the parts will print out properly. Almost all composers now use computers so they can save hours on the editing and printing process.

Why Call It Research?

There are good reasons for embracing the term research in regard to composition, as we seek a place for music as a discipline within the undergraduate research movement. Colleges and universities are placing increased emphasis on high-impact educational practices such as undergraduate research, and music majors risk losing out on central funding for research travel, recognition at awards ceremonies and at campus-wide celebrations of student achievement, by not participating as fully as possible. Sometimes works of this nature are called creativity, inquiry, or scholarship, but if a student is informed and deliberate about the process, calling it research encourages people in other fields to look at it through their own familiar lens. This can have the effect of raising credibility and respect from people in other parts of the academy. As musicians and music students, we often underestimate how much others already respect what we do, partly because many of them have tried, either successfully or unsuccessfully at earlier points in their lives, to read music, practice enough, or perform in front of an audience.

A slightly different way for composers to engage themselves in undergraduate research is to create interdisciplinary compositions. By combining their work with another, or perhaps several different areas of study, composers can create works that tie directly into other fields. When done properly, this can create a work of art with more depth and variety than a purely musical composition. One of the most common forms of interdisciplinary work in music is the conjunction of composition and film as a means for artistic creation. A motivated undergraduate music student can benefit by researching filmmaking techniques and create the visual portion for their work themselves. This is an actual exercise in some film scoring classes that music students take. Less common is the unification of composition and the sciences. Examples could include electrical engineering, mapping scientific data for its potential to control MIDI signals as well as to determine acoustic scores, or using programming languages for synthesis and MIDI control. Association with academics in other fields and the wider relevance of the work can benefit a composer by generating the interest of a larger audience for these works than only those involved in the world of music.

Consider the similarities between music and scientific disciplines; composition almost always incorporates organization of patterns as its framework. Patterns that may be described as "musical" can be found throughout mathematics, physics, the natural world, and more. Composers have drawn upon such resources before, and not only in modern times. For example, Amy Beach (1867–1944) successfully incorporated a transcription of a hermit thrush's call into a work for the piano. There are many other inspirations from nature, such as Debussy's *Oiseaux Tristes* (*Sad Birds*), George Crumb's *Vox Balaenae* (*Voice of the Whale*), *Peter and the Wolf* by Prokofiev, and *The Planets* by Gustav Holst.

An undergraduate composer/researcher would only need to discover or assign correlation between scientific findings and musical qualities to successfully integrate STEM (science, technology, engineering, and math) into composition-related projects. Possible ideas include: sampling sounds from the natural world and using the samples electronically or transcribing them; assigning pitches/dynamics/rhythmic value to data points; creating tone rows from mathematical sequences; or simply imitating the perceived feeling, mood, or emotion.

How to Document the Process and Why

To properly represent original musical composition as an undergraduate research area, it is important to be able to write about the process, just as a visual artist does in an artist statement accompanying an exhibition. This allows the casual observer to understand how an artist creates, including background research on a particular style, the techniques involved in the actual creation, and how it achieves the necessary balance of unity and variety, common to most art. Undergraduate research in music will necessarily be documented in a variety of ways depending on the topical area. Composition-related projects could culminate in program notes accompanying a live or recorded performance; an audio e-portfolio posted to a website; a lecture-recital; or a poster; or oral presentation at a conference. What is important is to explain the compositional decisions, the techniques used, stages of development, and the various ways that the project achieved the intended goals.

Evaluating a compositional research project naturally has a large subjective component. For this reason, criteria should include not only quality of the final product but a clear demonstration and documentation of the iterative process involved from start to finish. Understanding the process is not only an important lesson for the student, but it also allows the professor to better mentor the student, knowing some of the thought processes behind the compositional decisions. This mentoring relationship is one of the hallmarks of undergraduate research in most fields, and one of the things that make it so worthwhile and impactful.

Perspectives from Student Composers

The following statements are from Gregory Young's composition students when asked to respond in writing to the prompt, "What would constitute a real undergraduate research experience in composition for you?"

Junior Music Education/Music Technology Double Major Logan Henke:

Composition constitutes a research experience if done mindfully. I know that when I set out to compose a piece seriously, I have a question that needs to be answered. How can I manipulate my initial musical thought into the color/texture/instrumentation/form/etc. I desire? I draw upon my experience as a composer, the methods that I have been taught, and previous works which I admire or seek to emulate. The process of intentional composing requires research by its very nature. Often, hours of listening and studying are spent before a single note is placed on the page. Then, various processes are used to manipulate the music into the result that is most pleasing. These manipulations are learned and refined.

Senior Music Technology Major Mike Andrews:

Certainly, not all composition could be classified as research. The term research generally implies that one must reach a new conclusion by compiling information gathered from a variety of sources. In composition this could be considered the synthesis of styles and techniques amassed from the analysis of pre-existing music to create a work that is wholly new. In this way, one should not just show proficiency in imitating previous musical masters, but work to integrate varying styles in a way that shows a deep understanding of the music they have studied, as well as the involvement of high level critical thinking. This is extremely difficult to accomplish in a sincere way, and it is unlikely that an undergraduate student could contribute significantly to the musical language in an impactful way. Some composers use extra-musical sources such as geographic data, wifi signals, sounds from nature, or random chance to produce new sounds. This differs slightly from the assumption that most new music is derived from or influenced by previously composed music. Another way for composers to produce original research is through in depth study of technology as a means for music creation. With knowledge of programming languages, it is possible for composers to create new software processes for sound synthesis or unique electronic instruments to incorporate into their works. While this approach to compositional research could be seen as less musical and more technical, it still provides the possibility of significant advancements in how music is made and how our idea of timbre is expanded.

Samples of Abstracts Submitted to Conferences: Submitted to the 2016 World Congress of Undergraduate Researchers, Qatar

Impressions of Haiti for Guitar Ensemble

Anthony Gaglia, presenter; Gregory Young and Michael Videon, faculty mentors; Montana State University School of Music, Bozeman MT, 2016

The only Haitian composer whose music is included in the standard repertoire for classical guitar is Franz Casseus. Inspired by my work as a volunteer in Haiti in 2012, I plan to add to the repertoire for classical guitar ensembles within this cultural genre. After investigating the rhythms and harmonies of different Haitian genres I chose specific compositional techniques to capture what Haiti sounds like to me. This project involves composing an original piece for five guitars based on my research findings. The piece includes extended techniques for the guitar, some of which are original, as well as traditional techniques I have been studying during my degree program at MSU. I intend to capture the different parts of Haiti that inspire me including voodoo rituals and the work of Franz Casseus while being true to my compositional voice. The poster will document the research findings and the compositional process. To complement the poster I will provide a recording people can listen to as they study the score. MSU students will do this recording.

FIGURE 10.1 Antony Gaglia

Abstracts Submitted to the National Conference on Undergraduate Research

Orchestration of a Large-Scale Music Composition

Jordan Chase, presenter; Heather Gilligan, faculty mentor; Department of Arts & Humanities, Keene State College, Keene, NH, 2014

Writing a large-scale music composition is a process of creativity, research, hard work, and hours of dedication. This presentation will address the five main areas I focused on throughout my Summer Undergraduate Research Fellowship (commissioned grant) experience: instrumentation; orchestration; consideration of large-scale compositional form; the compositional process itself; and marketing and promotion of the piece. The study of instrumentation included time spent learning to play several of the orchestral instruments in order to help facilitate the development of idiomatic compositional ideas. Orchestration and formal structure were addressed by studying and listening to works by numerous composers of varying styles. The compositional process was a response to the studied topics as well as a daily creative endeavor. Composing was the focal point of the entire project. Throughout my speech I will address the many ways my ideas were created and developed. Marketing and promoting the piece entailed preparing the final score, entering national and international competitions, and contacting various conductors to potentially have my work performed. The presentation will conclude with a full play-back of my piece as well as a brief question-and-answer session.

Music Composition with Genetic Algorithms

Keaton R. Smith, presenter; Jeffrey Ward, Richard Fox, faculty mentors; College of Informatics, Computer Science Department, Northern Kentucky University, Highland Heights, KY, 2012

Human creativity has long been one of the most difficult things to emulate in the field of artificial intelligence. Musical composition is one particular example of a field requiring a great deal of effort to translate from the inspiration and unorganized thought that so often influences humans to the algorithmic format required to write a computer program to accomplish the same task. One potential method to do so is known as a genetic algorithm, which treats the formation of music in an evolutionary manner. To begin the process, a pool of simple music pieces is recombined and mutated to form a new generation of "child" compositions. These are then evaluated based on such criteria as rhythm, note sequences, and variability of pitch; the best compositions as determined by this scoring process go on to become "parents" of the next generation. This process continues until a specified number of cycles have been completed, at which point the best-scoring composition throughout the entire procedure is output as the final composition. This technique gives potential for much variability as well as retention of good characteristics of compositions, and could be considered as a viable approach to many other AI problems.

Cytoarchitecture: Music for Digital Improvisors

Greg Surges, author; Christopher Burns, advisor; Department of Music Composition/Technology, University of Wisconsin, Milwaukee, WI, 2009

2/8 Channel Software Instrument, April 2008 Realized in Pure Data— Computer Music Software Cytoarchitecture. The specific arrangement of cells in tissue, often used to refer to the arrangement of nerve cells in the cerebral cortex. The music is created by six computer improvisers, each monitoring and responding to musical output from the other five. Each module has a deliberately flawed memory, and incoming musical data is transformed and distorted according to the distinct character of that module. The modules all produce sound in personal ways, borrowing one synthesis algorithm from each decade between 1950 and 2008. The human performer listens and makes suggestions regarding the large-scale evolution of the piece, as well as the moment-to-moment ensemble relationships. The performance uses custom software designed for this piece. A messaging protocol was designed to allow for communication between the improvising modules. All synthesis and control takes place in real-time, creating a spontaneous musical experience for both audience and performer. A sample performance is found at the provided URL, and a 2 (or 8, if possible) channel sound system will be required for the performance.

Abstract Submitted to the 2006 State of North Carolina Undergraduate Research and Creativity Symposium

Lethargic Fervor

Jonathan D. Carter, author; Jennifer Snodgrass, mentor; Hayes School of Music, Appalachian State University, Boone, NC, 2006

The string quartet has evolved from a uniform, conventional genre of the Baroque era to an unconventional genre that focuses on off-centered melodies, disjunct countermelodies, and rhythmic deviations in meter and structure. This presentation will focus on the compositional techniques used in the creation of the string quartet entitled "Lethargic Fervor." Many styles are embraced within this composition including tonality, atonality, extreme dissonances, unconventional intervals, and chromaticism. After a performance of this composition using the Finale software system, the composer of this piece will offer the audience a in-depth analysis of the piece as well as added insight into the compositional process.

Abstract in the *Journal of Undergraduate Research,* University of Florida

J. S. Bach's Cello Suites: Composing an Idiomatic Equivalent for the Trombone

Alexander van Duuren, author; Arthur Jennings, mentor; Journal of Undergraduate Research, University of Florida, FL, 2008

Around the year 1720, J. S. Bach composed a series of six suites for solo violoncello. These suites are a very popular component of Bach's extensive repertoire and consequently have been transcribed for various instruments, including the trombone. However, since the performance capabilities of the cello differ greatly from those of the trombone, it is difficult or nearly impossible to play the suites in their original form. The purpose of this research was to compose an original, unaccompanied suite for the trombone that encapsulates both the essence of Bach's cello suites as well as idiomatic writing for the trombone. The product is a set of six movements (Prelude, Allemande, Courante, Sarabande, Bourrée I/II, and Gigue) in the Baroque style. The combination of technical exercises for the trombone with the popular and established style of Bach results in a musical etude that is interesting and effective.

Questions for Discussion

1 Why is it necessary to do an artist statement?
2 How long does a composition have to be and why?
3 Can material from published composers be used in a new composition?
4 How do I get my composition published?
5 Where can I find inspiration to start writing a composition?

11

INTERDISCIPLINARY PROJECTS

One could not better define the sensation produced by listening to music than to say that it is identical to that evoked by contemplation of the interplay of architectural forms. Goethe thoroughly understood this when he called architecture "frozen music."

Igor Stravinsky, *Chronicles of My Life*

Breakthrough innovation occurs when we bring down boundaries and encourage disciplines to learn from each other.

Gyan Nagpal, *Talent Economics*

Creativity, which I define as the process of having original ideas that have value, more often than not, comes about through the interaction of different disciplinary ways of seeing things.

Sir Kenneth Robinson, "Do Schools Kill Creativity"

Summary

This chapter will start out with an explanation of why some of the most exciting discoveries in recent times have occurred at the intersections of traditional disciplines. Important for undergraduates, is the lack of research that has been previously published linking music with other disciplines. This allows students to make original contributions that advance the knowledge base. Examples of successful interdisciplinary undergraduate research seminars are followed by suggestions for possible topics, and samples of student projects from journals and conferences. The conclusion will show the benefits many students and professors have enjoyed from such collaborations.

Why Two Different Disciplines?

The Survey Report from the 2016 annual meeting of the Global Research Council states "There is a wealth of literature arguing the important role interdisciplinary research has to play, particularly in addressing complex and societal challenges" (Gleed & Marchant, 2016).There is an increasing emphasis on finding solutions to some of these complex problems, or at least discussing ways they might be solved, in undergraduate curricula. In a recent article entitled "Pushing the Frontiers of Interdisciplinary Research: An Idea Whose Time has Come" there is a description of the bold initiatives at Stanford University and UC Berkeley that bring faculty together from different disciplines to aid in the discovery of knowledge (Gershon, 2000).

One fascinating example of an interdisciplinary discovery in the arts is the architectural design of the Eastgate shopping centre in Harare, Zimbabwe, that enables natural air conditioning modeled after giant termite mounds which use no external energy source, just great ventilation. This is described at Inhabitat.com, a weblog devoted to the future of design, tracking the innovations in technology, and practices and materials that are pushing architecture and home design towards a smarter and more sustainable future (Doan, 2012).

One of the biggest challenges in undergraduate research is finding a project that has not been done before. While faculty do not expect undergraduates to make significant contributions to a given discipline, many professors stress the importance of original student research, not simply repeating a study that is new to the student. To that end, choosing a project that examines an aspect of a discipline from the perspective of another discipline enables students to find topics not previously exhausted or explored in great depth. Many different subject areas in music intersect very well with many other disciplines. We naturally think of pairing music with disciplines such as art, language, literature, film, theatre, etc., but less obvious ones can be quite interesting, such as physics, medicine, sociology, anthropology, and psychology. Several pairs have proved fruitful in undergraduate seminars that link music with architecture, economics, and the brain, as outlined below.

London and the Lakes: Music and Economics from Handel to McCartney

At the launching of this seminar early in 2003, there was only one published book on the subject, entitled "Quarter Notes and Bank Notes" (Scherer, 2012). Therefore the two professors, Vince Smith and Gregory Young, knew that students would be able to find linkages between the two disciplines and specific topics that had not been examined. The semester of mentored research on these correlations culminated with a two-week study trip to London and the Lake

District, where the students led the group in explorations of the sites pertinent to their topics. A sample project, "The Music Composed for St. Paul's Cathedral," involved tracking the money that changed hands for commissioned works. The undergraduate researcher led the group on a tour of St. Paul's Cathedral during the trip, and explained his project. This educational guide model was used for several of the projects, on field trips to several different sites. Building upon the success of this seminar, a second seminar was offered and completed by 20 students, entitled "From the Vienna Woods to the Black Forest: Music and Economics in Vienna, Salzburg and Munich" (Young, 2008).

Music and the Brain

This seminar, co-taught by neuroscience professor John Miller, music professor Gregory Young, and licensed music therapist Shane Colvin, covered a wide variety of topics from music therapy to cognitive neuroscience. After background lectures from all three instructors on various relevant topics, students were required to conduct a research study in an area of their interest, present findings to the class, and write a 20-page paper. They were also encouraged to further disseminate their results at conferences where possible. Topics included:

- neuro-physical anomalies;
- efficacy of music therapy for concussions;
- dyslexia and music therapy;
- music and speech learning similarities and applications;
- use of musical keys/scales to evoke emotional responses;
- music therapy in Latino culture;
- music therapy for cancer patients;
- music therapy for sexual and domestic abuse/violence;
- effects of music on focus/attention in individuals with ADHD;
- using music to reveal subconscious memories/emotions.

The design for a Music and Sculpture seminar was inspired by the Musi-Tecture seminar described earlier, but in this case the students would pair up at the beginning of the course and create original music and sculpture pieces linked from the outset. A seminar on the music and literature of Wales was designed to include a culminating trip to Wales to study sites pertinent to student projects. Neither of these seminars has been taught yet, but could be done at any university.

Other Possible Seminars

There are many possibilities for similar undergraduate research seminars such as: linking art history and music history; similarities between music and language learning; computer science and music technology; correlations between music composition and dance choreography; or music theory and mathematics. Research seminar ideas that might not immediately come to mind are music and religious studies, comparisons of classicism in English literature and English music, aesthetic experiences in the fine arts, music, and politics, or biomimicry and music. An interesting exercise, either alone or in a group, is to come up with as many interdisciplinary seminars as possible that might work, and then try to come up with one or two that would not work. The second part of that exercise is tougher than one might think. This could be done in class with the students divided up into teams.

Suggestions for Possible Interdisciplinary Capstone Projects Involving Music

- Measure the physical properties of gut strings used in baroque performance practice vs. those of steel or nylon strings and research the reasons for these differences;
- compose music for an original student film;
- create a series of short tone poems based on a series of paintings by an art major;
- study the effects of mindfulness-based stress reduction on musical performance;
- have singers do yoga in their warm-up period and get their feedback about whether or not it is helpful;
- create a piece of furniture based on musical ideas accompanied by an artist statement;
- build a new instrument and document the construction process and the properties of the new creation—this could be done with engineering or architecture students, or both;
- combine singing bowls with traditional chamber instruments in performance;
- conduct focus groups on anxiety in musical performance vs. those giving speeches;
- work with an engineering student to design a working instrument, with acoustical calculations;
- examine correlations between the culinary arts and music;
- study the influence of musical notation on graphic design and vice versa;
- analyze the role of music in public transportation systems;
- document the devolution of gender bias in symphony orchestra auditions;
- study the patterns of music-related injuries, and/or their prevention;
- examine indigenous research methodology in community-based research;
- create musical themes to accompany an art exhibit.

Sample Undergraduate Abstracts

Language, Music, and Biological Evolution

Andrew Major, author; Jerome Bozeman, mentor; Montana State University; campus presentation; Bozeman, MT, 2014

This essay offers an in-depth review of the leading research on the evolution of language and music. At present, adaptationist theories suggest that language has been the direct target of natural selection for the adaptive value of expressing and comprehending complex propositions (Pinker & Jackendoff, 2005). In contrast, constructionist theories argue that there has only been indirect selection for language, providing humans with the social-cognitive capabilities to construct language (Tomasello et al., 2005). Regarding music, a number of adaptationist theories posit that the human capacity for music is a product of natural selection, implying a survival value of musical behaviors in our species' past (Wallin et al., 2000). In sharp contrast, a prominent nonadaptationist theory of music argues that music is a human invention and is biologically useless (Pinker, 1997). Finally, a recent theory by A.D. Patel suggests that music is a human invention, but can be biologically powerful and is theorized as a "transformative technology of the mind" (Patel, 2010).

The Mozart-Effect Revised: New Research Suggests that Learning to Play a Musical Instrument May Make You Smarter

Andrew Major, author; John Miller, mentor; Montana State University; Bozeman, MT, 2015

For the past two decades, Americans have been exposed to the well-intended idea that listening to Mozart or classical music will improve intellectual development in children and some claims include exposing the child to classical music while still *in utero*. A 1993 study investigated the effects of listening to the music of Mozart on spatial reasoning subtasks of the Stanford-Binet IQ test. Published in *Nature*, their results showed significant but temporary increases in spatial reasoning, the capacity to understand and remember the spatial relations among objects (as when children fit different shaped blocks into their respective complementary shapes), following exposure to a Mozart Sonata as compared to two other conditions of silence and verbal relaxation. While the results were taken out of context, the study described above opened the door to a new thread of research from interdisciplinary teams examining the effects music can have across a wide array of cognitive functions ranging from language learning to effects on IQ, a measure of intelligence. While many studies are inconclusive, faulted, or demonstrably wrong, some conclusions have emerged in recent years: 1) musical training has benefits that extend to non-musical areas of cognition and has effects on intelligence which are relatively small but long-lasting and are dose-dependent; 2) associations between musical training and intellectual abilities are general rather than restricted to specific aspects of intelligence; and 3) musical training is associated with increases in gray matter volume in motor, auditory, and visual–spatial brain regions.

The Perception of Pitch as Categorical Perception: Proposal for a Mismatch Negativity (MMN) Event-Related Potential (ERP) Study on the Perception of Pitch in Humans

Andrew Major, author; Charles Gray, mentor; Montana State University; Bozeman, MT, 2016

Current research has provided some evidence that pitch intervals act as learned sound categories in perception (Shepard & Jordan, 1984; Levitin, 1994; Dowling et al., 1995; Schellenberg & Trehub, 2003). Additionally, results of studies utilizing mismatch negativity (MMN) event-related potentials (ERP) have been consistent with this idea (Brattico et al., 2001; Trainor, McDonald & Alain, 2002). The proposed set of experiments will directly address whether pitch processing acts as categorical perception based on culturally learned musical systems, particularly due to culturally imposed musical scale structures, by analyzing the MMN produced by deviant pitch intervals in musicians and nonmusicians from varied cultural backgrounds. Results confirming that pitch processing acts as categorical processing will contribute to the body of evidence supporting generative models of functional brain architectures, where higher-level systems provide a prediction of the inputs to lower-level regions, by demonstrating that the brain maps acoustic variability onto stable mental categories to which incoming stimuli are compared.

Sample Abstracts Submitted to NCUR

Perceptions of Use of Hearing Protection in High String Musicians

Alyssa Adamec, author; Julia Bullard and Jaimie Gilbert, mentors; Department of Communication Sciences and Disorders, The University of Northern Iowa, Cedar Falls, IA, 2016

Noise-induced hearing loss (NIHL) is a common occupational disease (Griffin, 2009), especially in musicians. Violinists and violists are at particular risk due to the proximity of the instrument to the player's left ear. Research has shown high string players have a poorer threshold between 3000–6000Hz in their left ear compared to other orchestral players (Royster, 1991). They also have a risk of hearing loss due to their position in the orchestra (Sataloff, 2006). My research will focus on two questions: (1) how does wearing hearing protection impact a performer's experience; and (2) can high string players adjust to use of hearing protection? I will conduct an initial survey of violin and viola players, obtaining a foundational understanding of the participants regarding hearing loss, daily music exposure, and their perception of whether hearing loss is a problem. Next, I will provide a hearing test to participants. Finally, the participants will wear hearing protection over three weeks during solo practice and large ensemble rehearsals, completing surveys at the end of each week. These surveys will assess participants' perception of the experience of using hearing protection, and will also include qualitative self-assessment of key components of musicality: tone, intonation; practicing; and musical experience. My prediction is that the outcome of how musicians perceive their performance will influence whether they are able to adjust to ear protection. I am hoping to find minimal difference between their capability of playing scales with and without ear protection. By completing my research, my overall goal is to encourage more musicians to wear ear protection, allowing them to function in their profession longer. This project will also identify areas for further research, such as when the use of hearing protection should begin, and how students can be encouraged to wear hearing protection.

The Impact of Image: The Iconographic Celebrity of the Musician

Caroline Aylward, author; Maria Purciello, faculty mentor;
Department of Music, University of Delaware, Newark, DE, 2016

In today's pop culture, a musician's image is as important, if not more important than the music they create. This phenomenon is not as new as one might think, but rather dates from the Romantic period, when society began to view musicians as creative geniuses, rather than craftsmen. These musicians were held in such high regard that they were recognized as musical celebrities. Musical celebrity can be defined as an individual or group who represents the ideal of the period, has the 'It' factor, and can be associated with the following criteria: a sense of attraction to their creations from both sexes; self-confidence; and physical attraction though not necessarily beauty. These criteria derived from depictions of musicians publicly promote this celebrity status. As early as the nineteenth century, the portrayal of celebrity can be seen in the media of portraiture, photography, caricatures, and album artwork. Due to changing aesthetics over time, analyses of these media must consider the transition from passive to active inspiration, the study of physiognomy, the musician as a political figure, the effects of a musician's race and gender, as well as audience reception.

This paper uses iconography from various media to gain understanding of the developing form of musicians' popularity. It explores how the different facets of a musical celebrity have changed over time, and how those changes have led to a consideration of the notion of image versus talent that currently prevails in today's music industry. This research provides a new, multifaceted approach to linked notions of musicianship, musical innovation, and talent, as well as their affiliation with public perception via image.

Everyone's a Critic: Arts Criticism in the Digital Age

Scott Rohr, author; Marcela Kostihova, mentor; Department of English, Hamline University, Saint Paul, MN, 2009

The tradition of arts criticism has a storied and changing history. Renowned critics of the nineteenth century were alternately respected and feared, and had a disproportionate influence on the cultural mores of society. Today, the voices of criticism are more varied: new media have created an explosion of voices—amateur and professional alike—competing to find audiences for their writing. Even as traditional media—newspapers and periodicals among them—cut staffs of writers devoted to criticism (particularly classical music criticism), these same writers join cultural connoisseurs on the Internet, maintaining blogs about every matter of art and entertainment. This paper will examine how contemporary criticism exerts influence on American cultural production, how it attempts to define matters of taste, and ultimately, how today's consumer or audience is engaged and manipulated by these cultural commentators. While traditional journalists have real—perhaps even substantiated—anxiety about the their declining influence as arbiters of musical taste, the accompanying rise of the blogosphere provides a potential mitigation of that loss of coverage, at least quantitatively. This research explores the ways in which arts criticism is both enriched and degraded by the casual immediacy of writing online, as well as the potential for new audiences and previously unheard voices in criticism to meet, inform one another, and reinvent an increasingly moribund form. The results suggest a way for musicians and arts organizations to flourish in a challenging economic and cultural environment, perhaps preventing a collective hand wringing over the long-rumored death of classical music.

Conclusion

Interdisciplinary study is not only fascinating, but it is much more common in many fields, especially the sciences, than it has been in the past. Taking an interdisciplinary approach to capstone research projects involving music can provide students a less trodden path on which to make discoveries, an avenue for creativity, and a chance to add something meaningful to the current body of knowledge. Given the emphasis on interdisciplinary research in the twenty-first century, it also prepares students for a world in which collaboration and the interdependence of scholars are paramount.

Questions for Discussion

1   What might be some discipline pairings worth exploring?
2   Are there any discipline pairings that would NOT work as an interdisciplinary seminar?
3   Does this chapter generate new ideas based on interdisciplinarity?
4   Why is integrating interdisciplinary subjects into musical research important?

References

Bancroft, J., Young, G. & Sanderson, M. (1993). Musi-Tecture: Seeking useful correlations between music and architecture. *Leonardo Music Journal*, 3, 39–43.

Doan, A. (2012). Biomimicry's cool alternative: Eastgate centre in Zimbabwe. *Inhabit*. Retrieved from inhabitat.com/building-modelled-on-termites-eastgate-centre-in-zimbabwe/ (accessed 15 October 2016).

Gershon, D. (2000). Pushing the frontiers of interdisciplinary research: An idea whose time has come. *Nature*, 404, 313–315.

Gleed, A. & Marchant, D. (2016). Interdisciplinarity: Survey report for the Global Research Council. Retrieved from www.globalresearchcouncil.org/sites/default/files/pdfs/Interdisciplinarity%20Report%20for%20GRC_DJS%20Research.pdf (accessed 15 October 2016).

Scherer, F. (2012). *Quarter Notes and Bank Notes*. Princeton, NJ: Princeton University Press.

Young, G. (2008). Interdisciplinary undergraduate research in the arts and humanities at Montana State University, *CUR Quarterly*, 29(2), 30–32.

12

THE DISCOVERY OF KNOWLEDGE IN MUSIC HISTORY

If you learn music, you'll learn history. If you learn music, you'll learn mathematics. If you learn music, you'll learn most all there is to learn.

Edgar Cayce

Believe me when I say that some of the most amazing music in history was made on equipment that's not as good as what you own right now.

Jol Dantzig

If we look at music history closely, it is not difficult to isolate certain elements of great potency which were to nourish the art of music for decades, if not centuries.

George Crumb

Summary

Many students are required to write historical papers or honors theses in music history, and narrowing the topic based upon literature reviews is important. There are, however, many other possibilities for original work, including oral histories, biographies of local or regional composers, interdisciplinary work involving music history, research on cross-cultural influences, and music history research appropriate for program notes for a senior recital. The process for such research will be reviewed and contextualized for the undergraduate, with examples. Suggested topics will be outlined followed by sample abstracts and questions for discussion.

Introduction

Beethoven was right when he said "Music can change the world." Music has been changing the world and its history for centuries. But when and how did music start? How has music changed the world? What made the most influential composers that shaped the music of their day different from similar composers who are now forgotten? What kind of music did people listen to in different eras? How has that music contributed to what people listen to now? What is the future of music in the next few decades? Musicians around the world have pondered these questions as well as many others. Taking a narrow slice of one of these questions in a particular region or context could be the focus of a student research project.

Musicologists have researched the history of music for such a long time, and with so many publications, it is hard to find a subject within this broad category, suitable for an undergraduate research paper, especially in one semester. This chapter is designed to help students narrow down topic areas and suggest small projects that have not been done before. This allows students to make original contributions and thereby enhance the discipline, albeit in a small way. Whether it is an independent project with a topic chosen by the student or a small component of a music professor's larger research program, it is important to follow the process appropriate to the discipline that is followed by musicologists everywhere.

Process

Studying the literature in music history in a chosen subject area is critical before deciding on a topic for new research. This might involve typing topics into Google Scholar or other databases and critically examining the sources and the content. Wikipedia is not a reliable source of information, although sometimes the articles can have good sources cited in their bibliographies. Most universities have databases with peer-reviewed journals that are also great references. Websites such as NCUR (National Council on Undergraduate Research), BCUR (British Conference of Undergraduate Research), ACUR (Australian Conference of Undergraduate Research), and JUR (Journal of Undergraduate Research) from Colorado State University, can provide examples of completed undergraduate research in music history. Many resources are available, including interlibrary loan and the online resources that are annotated in Chapter 19. When narrowing and finalizing the topic, be sure and consult your professor, and have a look back at Chapter 3—Choosing Topics and Formulating Appropriate Research Questions.

Reasons for Researching Music History

Researching the history of music is a daunting task, so why do it? Well, examining the past can bring amazing revelations for the future. It is like looking through an old journal and realizing what you have learned and what you still need to learn. It can help in understanding the discipline broadly, and realizing that many new creations have been inspired and informed by prior masterworks. Seeing how William Byrd or Shostakovich wrote deep meaningful music under oppressive circumstances inspires composers to write new meaningful music in their own circumstances that can relate to their current audiences. Such history can inform performers and composers in a variety of ways. Researching how music first started as an oral tradition makes us appreciate the human voice. Even looking at how contemporary Christian music has progressed and regressed can help worship leaders and musicians write and sing songs that are meaningful and appropriate on Sunday mornings. Looking back at music in the past helps us to see what kind of experimentations could help move the discipline forward. Lastly, music history is important because it gives listeners an understanding of context. Listening to the orchestral piece "Hoedown" by Aaron Copland will be a much better experience if one knows its place in the ballet (*Rodeo*), the story, the choreography, and the context.

Possible Topics

- Study newer contemporary music (Native American music, African American music, etc.), its origins, and potential for future practices;
- investigate newer instruments and how they built on previous ideas;
- learn how traditional instruments have changed over the years;
- interview and/or write about local and/or lesser-known artists, composers, or teachers;
- conduct and/or examine oral and written histories;
- search for unknown composers' works;
- research old instruments and new practices with those instruments;
- write about modern composers who have won competitions;
- analyze music from other aspects of the performing arts, such as musical theater;
- look into the history of pit orchestras over the last 50 years;
- find new genres of music, such as Bright Sheng's compositions (Sheng, n.d.)
- scrutinize the music of Pulitzer Prize winners (Pulitzer Prizes, n.d.);
- study new composition styles and movements;
- explore the history of different music cultures in your region;
- research television and radio music;
- study music abroad in tandem with an ensemble concert tour;
- locate and interview a local band and/or ensemble;
- discover facets of electronic music and its impact;
- read up on the history of the campus music building and share your perspective;

- research different historical acoustic settings for performance;
- find out about the history of the local marching band;
- study the national anthems from around the world;
- focus on specific topics in a composer's piece, such as the folk and nonfolk elements in Bartok's Two Fantasies for Violin and Piano;
- understand the history of rubato in Romantic pieces;
- analyze selected guitar works in terms of their historical context;
- search for ethnic influences, such as Jewish music in Mahler's Symphony No. 2;
- look at women's place in professional music making;
- analyze the evolution of Broadway show songs;
- interview a graduate from the Juilliard historical performance degree program (Juilliard School of Music historical performance website);
- interview a music history professor about his/her research area;
- research jazz music programming at your university and its evolution;
- compare and contrast two or more music history textbooks, what eras/composers does each book emphasize?

Sample Abstracts Submitted to NCUR

www.cur.org/conferences_and_events/student_events/ncur/archive/

A New Approach: The Feminist Musicology Studies of Susan McClary and Marcia J. Citron

Kimberly Reitsma, author; Sandra Yang and Lyle Anderson, mentors; Music and Worship Department, Cedarville University, Cedarville, OH, 2014

The goal of this project is to determine the extent to which the women's movement in America influenced the approaches which Susan McClary and Marcia J. Citron have taken in their musicological studies. Some of the feminist ideologies I will be discussing in McClary's and Citron's works include: social equality between male and female; acceptance of what culture recognizes as "feminine" qualities; and the elimination of what culture recognizes as "masculine" qualities. Susan McClary has produced numerous research publications in these areas as they relate to music. Her book which launched feminist musicology was *Feminine Endings*, published in 1991. The title refers to the traditional usage in music theory of the terms "masculine" and "feminine" to describe certain cadences as strong or weak. The feminist musicology approach is not limited to the analysis of music composed by women, but it has also been useful in analyzing works by men. Susan McClary has used this approach while studying Beethoven's Fifth

Symphony and Bizet's *Carmen*. Marcia J. Citron also has contributed numerous publications in this field. She published an essay in 1992 entitled, "Feminist Approaches to Feminist Musicology," in which she discusses various feminist approaches which have been taken in analyzing different types of music. Within this essay, she shares her interest in the application of women-centered theories and ideologies to absolute, as opposed to programmatic, music. In her book, *Gender and the Musical Canon*, Citron has also done research on the psychological effect which stereotypical gender views have upon women composers. In spite of the popular reception of their works, both McClary and Citron acknowledge that this new field of feminist musicology deserves much more research. This subject is vitally important as today's musicians increasingly evaluate the effects of social movements upon the music and music scholarship of a particular time and culture. This investigation goes beyond music itself by including other disciplines, such as sociology and psychology, to further understand musicology. Through my research, I expect to demonstrate that Susan McClary and Marcia J. Citron have significantly expanded the scope of contemporary musicology through their application of feminist theory.

The Dies Irae ("Day of Wrath") and the Totentanz ("Dance of Death"): Medieval Themes Revisited in Nineteenth-Century Music and Culture

Erin Brooks, author; Elizabeth Markham, faculty mentor; Department of Music; Inquiry: The University of Arkansas Undergraduate Research Journal *Vol. 4, 2003*

During the pivotal November 2002 football game of Arkansas vs. Georgia in the SEC conference championship, the Georgia marching band struck up their defensive rallying song. Instead of a typical "defense" song, the band played an excerpt of the Gregorian sequence *Dies Irae* ("Day of Wrath ") from the Roman Catholic Requiem Mass. Drastically dissociated from its original medieval milieu, this musical sequence still manages to elicit the same effect of fear and foreboding nearly a thousand years later. Precisely because of its deep musical and cultural roots, the *Dies Irae* occupies a significant place in history, closely intertwined from early on with the medieval folk motif *Totentanz* ("Dance of Death"), widely depicted in medieval art, and dramatically revived in nineteenth-century music, art, and literature. This multidisciplinary study focuses on the history of art and music of these two medieval themes during their development, and then moves on to study them in nineteenth-century culture. Specifically, the manipulation of the original Gregorian chant and the incorporation of the idea of a medieval dance are analyzed in the music of Hector Berlioz, Franz Liszt, and Camille Saint-Saëns. Numerous other contextual links are explored as well, such as Johann Wolfgang von Goethe, Victor Hugo, Henri Cazalis, William Blake, and Alfred Rethel, all of whom created nineteenth-century artistic or literary masterpieces derived from the thematic seeds of the *Dies Irae* and the *Totentanz*. Although neither of these ideas endured in their original form during the Romantic era, the inherently compelling nature of these themes that center on the macabre but inevitable end of life captivated the Romantic geniuses and continue to intrigue us to this day.

Undergraduate Research Journal Abstracts

Perspectives in Music

Helena Gandra, Apollon Undergraduate EJournal, *Issue 4, 2014*

This paper is divided into three parts: in Chapter 1, I will be exploring the definition of silence, the difference between silence, sound and music and how is it represented in music tradition; in Chapter 2, I will be defining Wagner's musical aesthetics and the role that silence plays in Wagner's work *Tristan and Isolde*'s overture; finally in Chapter 3, I will determine Cage's musical aesthetics and the role that silence plays in his piece "4'33"." Relationships and comparisons will be established between the two composers and their philosophy of music, as well as their social and political context. In more general terms, I will raise questions regarding the ontology of silence and music. Indeed, I will be reflecting on the role of silence in reshaping a new understanding of music.

The methodology utilized in this thesis is qualitative and therefore, I will approach the study of musical works and their comparison from a musical, philosophical, historical, and socio-political perspective. In terms of literature review, the information acquired in relation to Cage and silence was very useful and easy to find since there are so many writings on the subject. However, gathering information on Wagner and silence was a harder task, as it is not a usual topic in the studies of his work. I, therefore, tried to combine facts with my critical response to the information obtained.

Sa'ad Zaghlul's Gramophone: The Effects of Popular Music on the Egyptian Nation

Haley Britt Beverburg, Stanford University Intersect, The Stanford Journal of Science, Technology & Society, *2016*

Egyptian music was affected by, and had a significant effect on, Egyptian politics, economics, and society prior to the 1919 revolution. In this paper, I explore the diverse musical traditions of Egyptian populations in the era prior to the fall of the Khedivate to give context to the changes that occurred during the years of the British Protectorate and World War I. I highlight the democratizing effect that the introduction of new recording technologies had on Egyptian society, demonstrating that the marketization of musical culture in many ways homogenized what was previously a culturally diverse population. Finally, I argue that the social networks created by popular song allowed Egyptians of all backgrounds to construct and participate in a public national consciousness, creating an environment ripe for the 1919 revolutions and the independence movement that followed.

Conclusion

The possibilities for topics to choose from in the category of music history are virtually limitless. Three semesters of music history are required in most degree programs in the predominantly English-speaking countries covering mainly Western music. There are also many different kinds of music in the world with thousands of different instruments not generally included in classical orchestras and bands (see Chapter 17, Ethnomusicology, Culture, and Popular Music). The hardest part is finding a topic that is interesting, but not overly researched. The history of music from a specific region, for example, would be a good research topic. Most likely a biography of a little-known regional composer would be an original contribution. That is what music history is, stories about people making the music that brings something new into the world, one person at a time. The tagline for the American Composers Forum's Composers' Datebook is "reminding you that all music was once new" (American Composers Forum, n.d.).

Questions for Discussion

1   Does our perspective change over time?
2   How is knowledge in music history created?
3   How does knowledge of music history influence performers?
4   Why is interest increasing in historical performance practice?
5   What kinds of music history projects involve physical measurements?
6   Will electronic media replace live performers?

References

American Composers Forum. (n.d.). Celebrating 15 years of Composers Datebook. Retrieved from https://composersforum.org/discover/articles/celebrating-15-years-composers-datebook (accessed 23 October 2016).

Juilliard School of Music. (n.d.). Historical performance. Retrieved from www.juilliard.edu/degrees-programs/music/historical-performance (accessed 23 October 2016).
Pulitzer Prizes. (n.d.). Prize winners by year: music. Retrieved from www.pulitzer.org/prize-winners-by-category/225 (accessed 4 November 2016).
Sheng, B. (n.d.). Bright Sheng, composer, conductor and pianist. Retrieved from http://brightsheng.com/bio.html (accessed 5 November 2016).

13

MUSIC THEORY

We must see that music theory is not only about music, but about how people process it. To understand any art, we must look below its surface into the psychological details of its creation and absorption.

Marvin Minsky, "Music, Mind and Meaning"

Music is the one incorporeal entrance into the higher world of knowledge which comprehends mankind but which mankind cannot comprehend.

attributed to Ludwig van Beethoven

Summary

Although music theory, analysis, and aesthetics are more likely to be topic areas for faculty research projects, here might be an opportunity for a win–win situation in which an undergraduate music major working alongside a professor shares a mutual benefit. Other student-directed projects could focus on the way students perceive the study of music theory, how they overcome obstacles, how they respond to certain pedagogical practices, etc. Still others could explore new apps and websites to help high school students prepare to be successful music majors, as theory is often a barrier course or a hurdle for many. Other suggestions for topics and published undergraduate abstracts of both qualitative and quantitative studies will be followed by questions for discussion.

What Is Music Theory?

In simple terms, music theory is a system used to explain music and its construction. Music theory can be used to analyze almost any piece of music. It can convey simple information such as how fast a piece progresses harmonically, to complex concepts such as interlocking rhythms and hexachordal combinatoriality. Anything written on a sheet of music is called music notation, and the techniques or practices used to describe or explain how it is composed can be considered music theory.

The study of music theory is essential to a musician's ability to understand and perform a piece in the way the composer originally intended. Music composition is practically impossible without it. A music theorist who can't read music is like a historian who can't read or write their own native language. They are still able to learn the information associated with their field, and are able to convey it to others, but there are severe limits on what they are able to study and their ability to explain difficult concepts to others without visual aid.

The theory of musical notation is the lifeblood of analysis. It enables us to study and learn about the construction of any piece of music regardless of whether it is a chant from hundreds of years ago, or an atonal piece that was commissioned last year. Even if it is not written down, aural skills can help with a theoretical analysis. A good music teacher will begin teaching their students music notation and the basics fundamentals of theory as early as general music in elementary school, giving students the foundation to continue learning over the course of their entire pre-college education. Once a student graduates and begins to study music full time at university, the expectations for music theory knowledge immediately increase.

Music Theory in the Undergraduate Curriculum

For many music students, music theory presents a challenge unlike other areas of music study, and a minority of music majors seems to like it, while the rest either just tolerate it or find it frustrating. Like mathematics, certain people seem predisposed to do well in music theory, for it clearly puts demands on left-brain skills. Most music degree curricula require two years of music theory and a semester of form and analysis. Further courses such as counterpoint, arranging, and orchestration are often offered as electives. To prepare for the first semester of music theory as a music major in college, students should be able to read treble and bass clefs, and have a working knowledge of chords, scales, and arpeggios.

The teaching and learning aspects of music theory are interesting, and they parallel mathematics in that there are new ways of teaching the same material that are disseminated from time to time. Technologies to help with music theory learning are increasingly available for little to no cost, including new computer applications and software freely available on the Internet.

If a senior capstone project in music theory is conducted as a part of a faculty research project, the student might help with a literature search, help conduct surveys, or analyze sections of compositions pertinent to the topic. An independent student project in theory, in order to be original, might test perceptions of learning, or actual learning outcomes using a particular new app or web tool, conduct focus groups about the use of particular pedagogical tools, invent a game to teach a particular concept, or examine and analyze a local composer's piece that has never been analyzed by a third party. Additional suggestions follow.

Possible Topics for Research in Music Theory

- Analyze a piece of music that is out of print, with no available analyses;
- explore ways that aleatory music can be analyzed;
- study metrical dissonance in the music of specific composers;
- rewrite a piece of music with complex meter changes and compare the two;
- research when the different "rules" of music theory were written;
- study the differences between an original composition and its arrangement;
- research why some music majors dislike studying theory;
- investigate effects of early education in music theory, at different levels;
- explore the different ways of scaffolding music theory skills and decide which ones work best for teaching new students;
- compare different mobile applications and websites related to music theory instruction and explanation, discuss the merits and drawbacks of each;
- connect music theory with other studies such as math or science;
- review the extent to which music theory is keyboard-based, explore alternate ways to learn music theory;
- investigate the influences of music theory knowledge on the interpretation of different works, and how it might inform music performance;
- explore ways that music theory can enhance instruction in a private studio setting;
- do qualitative research on why some studio teachers do not teach any music theory, ask for tips from the ones who do;
- collect and summarize resources for teaching theory as part of studio instruction;
- research how the application of music theory affects singers' intonation;
- compare the music theory programs at different universities, materials studied, what is and is not required for different degrees, etc.;
- study which schools require the teaching of 12-tone music analysis and discuss different viewpoints about it;
- come up with a new way music can be analyzed or organized;
- examine the correlation between standardized test scores and success in music theory;
- experiment with a peer-mentoring program for music theory;

- do a meta-analysis of Google reviews of music theory textbooks;
- interview music theory teachers to discover and document pedagogical tool;
- see if an app like DuoLingo (for language) could be a model for a music theory app.

Sample Abstracts Submitted to NCUR

www.cur.org/conferences_and_events/student_events/ncur/archive/

IV-V-I: The Use of a Games-Based Learning Approach to Understanding Harmonic Function in Music Theory

Alexander M. Alberti, author; Jennifer Snodgrass, mentor; Music Department, Appalachian State University, Boone, NC, 2013

The mastery of harmonic function is one of the most important concepts in the early stages of traditional music theory curriculum in both high school and collegiate music education. Lack of understanding in this area can cause issues that follow a student through the remainder of their curriculum. Educators are always looking for new ways to help students understand the concept of function, and ingrain it not just into memory for a few short months, but into applicable practice for the rest of their musical lives. The card game "IV-V-I" is a music theory card game designed by Rafael Hernandez to help students reinforce and develop an understanding of harmonic motion within the context of a phrase, highlighting traditional function, voice leading, special harmony, historical concepts in music, part writing, and cadences. Games-based learning approaches have proven effective in the new generation of learners who thrive on social interaction, peer learning, and social constructivism. Could IV-V-I be a suitable supplement to help students grasp and retain the concepts of harmonic function? This pilot study took place at a regional university with students in an introductory theory course for music industry majors – a degree track often overlooked in the field of theory. During a unit on harmonic function, a pre-test was given after several days of instruction to measure students understanding of the concept. Afterward, a group of students, comprised of half the class, were instructed on game-play and freely given IV-V-I to participate. After two sessions of playing the game, a post-test was given to measure student growth and understanding of harmonic function. This presentation will focus on the results of the study, and methods to integrate IV-V-I into the music theory classroom.

Music Theory and Aural Skills: Creating a Crossroads Between Context and Mastery

Meredith Anderson, author; Jennifer Snodgrass, mentor; School of Music, Appalachian State University, Boone NC, 2012

Within the typical classroom on both the K-12 and university level, there exists a disconnect in the methods of teaching music theory and aural skills. In the middle and high school music classroom, written music theory is simplified and compressed, giving future music students a skewed and sometimes incorrect view of the subject. Aural skills, on the other hand, could be considered more productive on the K-12 level, being taught completely within context. At the university level, written theory is taught in great depth, dissecting pieces of music that the students would otherwise never see. However, aural skills are dictation-based and rarely put into context. This disconnect causes a vicious cycle in the world of music education. Students start their musical training in the K-12 classroom, "mastering" music theory and aural skills in compressed but contextual ways. Some students then move on to a university music program as music education majors, studying theory and aural skills in great depth, but out-of-context. When these students graduate, most return to the K-12 classroom as teachers. This is problematic because these students do not understand how to integrate their university theory training in a public school classroom. There are many ways that university faculty and public school teachers can work together to provide a smooth transition for students between public school and the university and back, specifically in terms of theory and aural skills instruction. Based on observations of aural skills instruction at both the university and K-12 levels, this presentation will offer qualitative data in terms of concepts being taught on various levels and how each can be more balanced in order to create a collective learning experience between instructor and future music educators.

Steel Drums as an Alternative to the Piano in the Field of Music Theory Pedagogy

Duncan Boatright, author; Jennifer Snodgrass, mentor; Hayes School of Music, Appalachian State University, Boone, NC, 2012

In the field of music theory pedagogy, the piano can be an extraordinarily useful tool. Instructors are able to use the piano to demonstrate to their students any melodies, pitches, or chords that they wish. In addition to this application, every music theory student is trained to relate their entire knowledge of music theory to a piano keyboard. A typical undergraduate music student, when asked to name a pitch a certain musical interval above a given pitch, will visualize a piano and use the keyboard to determine their answer. All musicians tend to think in the smallest common musical interval, a half step, which also happens to be the interval between adjacent keys on a piano keyboard. The purpose of this research is to determine if an alternative instrument, particularly a steel drum, can serve the same purpose without hindering a student's learning process. In some areas of the world, a piano may not be as commonplace as the popular folk instruments of the particular region. In Trinidad and Tobago, for example, steel drums can be found on every street corner, whereas pianos can be a rare sight. Using an alternative instrument as a means of music theory instruction could benefit students in these areas in incredible ways. Adjacent notes on a steel drum, depending on the particular instrument, are separated by the musical interval of a perfect fifth. Because the perfect fifth is so integral to so many areas of music theory, it is the belief of some that this instrument could serve the same purpose as a keyboard in providing a foundation for students to build their knowledge. This research also hopes to determine whether or not it is possible to eliminate any sort of an aural bias towards the piano in the fields of musical ear training and aural skills. Undergraduate students, after years of ear training with a piano, tend to hear pitches produced by a piano easier than pitches produced by other instruments. It would follow, then, that if students train their ears using an instrument such as a steel drum, they would then exhibit an aural bias towards the steel drum. This presentation will conclude with a brief demonstration of music theory instruction using a steel drum.

Published Undergraduate Abstracts

Vibha Agarwala (2011) Music + Architecture: The Spatial Translation of Schenkerian Analysis University of Florida Journal of Undergraduate Research 13(1). http://ufdc.ufl.edu/ UF00091523/0060 (accessed 30 November 2016)

Architecture and music share unexplored design and analytic frameworks. In tonal music, Schenkerian Analysis is a method that demonstrates the hierarchy of the composition's musical structure. This methodological approach provides an understanding of the composition's most basic framework and its most refined ornamentation. This paper argues that reductive analysis can be applied to architecture to generate a similarly systematic approach in the design process. Ultimately, reductive analysis can be used to develop new methodologies in the process of design.

David Godbold (2014) The Theory of Music: Warp Speed. The Carthage Vanguard 1(1). www.carthage.edu/live/files/2491-the-carthage-vanguard-volume-ipdf (accessed 30 November 2016)

Warp Speed, composed by David Godbold, is a perpetual motion composition consisting of repetitive ostinato figures and fanfares. This article breaks down Warp Speed into music theory and musical thematic structures. Within this article, the reader will understand how Warp Speed was constructed through the use of music theory.

Conclusion

Music theory is the backbone upon which music stands. Though many dislike the more unmusical aspects of theory, such as analysis, it is undeniable that its study informs musicians in more ways than they realize. Music is constantly changing and adapting with culture, and the theory behind it is changing as well. Perhaps the most important thing to research is not music theory itself, but rather what the most effective ways to study it are. Realizing a musician's true potential is harder without the understanding that comes from music theory study.

Questions for Discussion

1 What is the relative importance of music theory with respect to other areas and why?
2 Does a good musician need to know music theory?
3 Why is it important to study music theory?
4 Why can studying music theory be difficult for people, even if they have been around music for a long time?
5 How does the study of music theory influence performance?
6 How is music theory changing today?

14

MUSIC EDUCATION

Music is a moral law. It gives soul to the universe, wings to the mind, flight to the imagination, and charm and gaiety to life and to everything.

attributed to Plato

Music education opens doors that help children pass from school into the world around them a world of work, culture, intellectual activity, and human involvement. The future of our nation depends on providing our children with a complete education that includes music.

Gerald Ford

Music education can help spark a child's imagination or ignite a lifetime of passion. When you provide a child with new worlds to explore and challenges to tackle, the possibilities are endless. Music education should not be a privilege for a lucky few, it should be a part of every child's world of possibility.

Hillary Clinton

Music enhances the education of our children by helping them to make connections and broadening the depth with which they think and feel. If we are to hope for a society of culturally literate people, music must be a vital part of our children's education.

Yo-Yo Ma

With the growing popularity in e-learning, it occurred to me that the e should mean more than electronic. If we are going to call it e-learning, shouldn't it be effective, efficient, and engaging?

M. David Merrill, *The First Principles of Instruction*

Summary

This chapter opens with a rationale for undergraduate research in music education. Benefits specific to pre-service teachers include enhanced abilities to make informed instructional decisions, improved attitudes toward music content, and changes to the way pre-service teachers plan to teach in their future classrooms. An examination follows about the need to re-classify teaching portfolios, often required in teacher education programs, as research. This is followed by an overview of relevant topics in music education along with representative samples. Topics include the evaluation of teaching effectiveness, pedagogical issues and the measurement of student learning, the National Core Arts Standards, students with special needs, classroom management, motivation and retention, early childhood issues, and advocacy (Harney & Young, 2016).

Introduction

Picasso once said in a *Time* interview, "Every child is an artist. The problem is how to remain an artist once we grow up." The same may be true for curiosity, so it is imperative that we nurture curiosity in all students and impress upon them the variety of paths toward the discovery of knowledge, namely research. Planting the seeds of inquiry within the context of education from an early age seems like an obvious first step toward creating a culture of research and discovery. Students majoring in education are notably underrepresented in undergraduate research programs. The first earned doctorate of Music Education was in 1895 (Phelps 1983, p. 2) Therefore, embedding research skills, experiences, and opportunities within teacher preparation programs seems equally obvious." Recent studies have shown that such skills and experiences can improve students' attitudes about music content, and enhance their approaches when it comes to pedagogy.

Should the Teacher Work Sample Be Counted as Research?

During the semester of student teaching, an action research project is usually required. The Teacher Work Sample, sometimes called EdTPA or generically, the lesson plan unit project, is the research project student teachers have to finish before they graduate. It is a project that guides future teachers through lesson planning, learning about classes as a whole, and conducting some very basic research. Since some college students need to complete their capstone undergraduate research class before student teaching, this can create great opportunities to further develop the scaffolding of research skills to enhance the subsequent project. Even though a Teacher Work Sample may not seem like real research, there are many aspects one can take from their undergraduate research to enhance their Teacher Work Sample. Should a Teacher Work Sample be classified as research? Are there aspects of undergraduate research that should be emphasized to improve students Teacher Work Sample (Harney & Young, 2016)?

Using Technology and Applications, How Can Students and Teachers Discover and Learn?

Technology is becoming increasingly intertwined in our everyday life. There are many opinions about technology. Some do not like its dominance, and some are using it to its advantage. In music and other subjects, teachers are giving their students laptops, iPads, and even letting them use their own phone to download applications to help their learning. There are music teachers across the U.S. using applications, such as Smart Music, or MusicTheory.net to help their students learn in their class. One could study how these music applications being used, or how other internet sites such as www.curiosity.com and www.lumosity.com could have potential for future teachers. In the music classroom, what other kinds of applications are available to help students learn musical concepts? What kinds of applications are there to help students create music? What are the pros and cons of using technology and applications in the music classroom? Are college music education curricula changing to reflect the latest brain research? Because change is so rapid in this realm, capstone projects can fairly easily be original research.

Just Discover Something!

Discover something new! The field of music education affords many opportunities for undergraduates with a little creativity to choose a research project with at least a new perspective. Research something or someone locally. Where do incoming music education students come from in your state, and what might influence that? These days, what are student perceptions as they choose which instrument they would like to learn? Do they differ from perceptions a generation ago? Do educators influence students' choices in instruments? How can new teachers learn to balance their band and orchestra without having a bias toward certain instruments? How do different schools, Montessori, home school, private/public, teach and view music education differently?

At the beginning of her senior year at Montana State University (2016), Hannah Lane was given the opportunity to teach music to 3–6-year-olds at a local Montessori. Montessori schools are different from public and private schools when it comes to teaching students, with a focus on individualized learning for each student. In music, she taught the 3–6-year-olds the same material, without much individualized learning. As a class they enjoyed making music together. Coming into the Montessori setting, she did not educate herself on how to properly teach in a Montessori setting, using what she had learned in her college classes to conduct the lessons, but she learned a lot about herself as a teacher the more she taught. Having not studied music pedagogy for 3- and 4-year-olds, she guided herself through it. How is music education different in Montessori schools compared to public schools? How can music educators in the Montessori setting incorporate more of the goals and ideas of the Montessori? Should there be separate training when a music educator first comes into the Montessori setting? Although her senior capstone project was contributing to this chapter, several of the above questions, or a few in combination, could also have served as a topic for her senior capstone project.

Why Is Research in Music Education Needed?

The potential impacts of undergraduate research in music education have not been thoroughly studied, but one could surmise that teachers would be better prepared to stimulate a quest for creativity and discovery in their future students if they had the experience themselves. "Students who have opportunities to engage in undergraduate research have significantly better learning outcomes than similar students without those opportunities" (Manak & Young, 2014). Capstone research projects can examine the various facets of education, both quantitatively and qualitatively. Most future teachers have opportunities for this, whether in a project like the teacher work sample or a similar action research component of student teaching. In a research project conducted by Kristin Harney and Gregory Young, they found that what students learn in their teacher work sample—comparing pre- and post-tests, self-reflection, measuring processes, implementing a plan, planning informed by standards, and identifying contextual factors – will transfer into their own classroom on their first job (Harney & Young, 2016).

Recently the Council on Undergraduate Research (CUR) started a new division for education. Surprisingly, most disciplinary areas were already represented, and it begs the question, "Why is education, a field that could serve as an umbrella for all undergraduate teaching, be one of the last divisions within CUR?" The answer lies mainly in the fact that departments of education focus primarily on preparing future teachers, and their curricula are so full of requirements from accreditation and public instruction mandates, that they did not think they had room for an undergraduate research requirement. However, when one takes a close look at what teachers study, what projects they have to complete, and the importance of them passing on the magic of discovery to their future students, it made perfect sense to start this new CUR division. Another factor in this equation is that faculty have the ability to alter the curriculum slightly and make research part of the standard curriculum for education majors if they so choose.

Music Education Correlates with Other Fields

Music education research does not have to strictly focus on music and music education only. One can broaden the topic and see interdisciplinary potential with a variety of other fields. The National Association for Music Education (NAfME) gives these topic ideas:

- music education and brain development;
- music education and math/spatial reasoning;
- music education and reading/verbal skills;
- music education and academic achievement;
- music education and successful schools;
- music education and social and emotional development;
- music education and academic achievement.

Where Can Music Education Majors Get More Information?

There are many resources from which future teachers can get information about teaching. Most states have an annual music education conference programmed specifically for teachers with two full days of professional development sessions, and music education majors are welcome. Often they have their own student chapter. There are also national conferences with internationally recognized speakers and facilitators. Video programs, blogs, journals, and many other resources are out there that provide information. Organizations, like the National Association of Music Educators, have lots of information on their website as well as monthly emails that are full of information across all musical disciplines. Other websites, annotated in Chapter 19 of this book, include the American Choral Directors Association, the American School Band Directors Association, College Orchestra Directors Association, and others. The Music Teachers National Association is a great source for teachers and students. Students and teachers can sign up to receive magazines in the mail or electronically. Current and former teachers and colleagues can be a great source of information and experience with whom to share thoughts and ideas.

Possible Topics

- Study the Mark O'Connor method for violin and other new pedagogical methods;
- study the feasibility of private lessons via distance through live video;
- examine the feasibility of a local children's opera chorus program;
- look into outreach programs research different models, and their feasibility for other universities;

- research surrounding universities to design a curriculum for music therapy;
- explore different learning styles in private lessons:
  - visual (spatial);
  - aural (auditory-musical);
  - verbal (linguistic);
  - physical (kinesthetic);
  - logical (mathematical);
  - social (interpersonal);
  - solitary (intrapersonal);
- examine the role of mindfulness in classroom management;
- teaching music to children with special needs:
  - how can teachers include children with special needs into the music classroom, and what ways of inclusion work best?
- focus on different learning styles to teach different topics:
  - are there certain music ideas that are taught best by focusing on one teaching style – visual, aural, verbal, physical, logical, social, and solitary?
- research how to keep students motivated using different tools:
  - what teaching tools can be used to keep students motivated and engaged in the music setting?
- use field experience to test pedagogy:
  - while in general music, instrumental, and choral methods, students should use that time to explore and test out different pedagogical methods;
- survey fellow music majors about perceptions of music education;
- research reasons for high teacher turnover rates;
- interview long-standing successful music educators:
  - ask some established music educators what has been their motivation for being in the field for so long. What works for them? Why have they been teaching for so long?
- discover reasons for choosing music education—survey incoming music education majors;
- conduct focus groups with alumni who are teaching and have had undergraduate research—finding out how it helps in their teaching;
- examine how Myers Briggs predicts student choice of music education as a major:
  - with the results of the Myers Briggs personality test, are there correlations between results and teaching styles/views?

Sample Abstracts Submitted to NCUR

www.cur.org/conferences_and_events/student_events/ncur/archive/

Adolescent Perspectives on the Emotional, Social, and Behavioral Impacts of Participation in Music Education: An Ethnographic Study at Mountain View High School

Johanna S. Nilsson, author; Kathleen Modrowski, faculty mentor; Department of Global Studies, Long Island University, New York, 2016

This study examines adolescent perceptions of the emotional, social, and behavioral benefits of participation in a choir at Mountain View High School, in Mountain View, CA. Current and former students and parents identified over 99 variables, or impacts, that they believe choir had on its members, including: increased ability to recognize and correct mistakes; to accept and apply constructive criticism; to negotiate and compromise with peers; and to interact in a variety of social situations. Additionally, students reported positive emotional impacts, such as an increase in self-confidence and willingness to take risks. These findings could have ramifications for the future of music education, as educators integrate social values into their curricula and use music as a tool to affect students' abilities to interact in the world.

The Effect of Music Education on Social and Political Liberalism in High School and College Students

Alexander M. Alberti, author; William L. Pelto, mentor; Hayes School of Music, Appalachian State University Boone, NC, 2012

Bullying is an issue that has, for decades, run rampant throughout our nation's youth, stemming from intolerance and ignorance of race, nationality, religion, or sexuality. Newspaper headlines are lighting up with news of suicide attempts and beatings among high school students, reaching even up into the ranks of collegians. Rallies are popping up across the United States to revoke and prohibit rights to many citizens, based off of conservative ideals. However, in music classrooms across the nation at all levels, students who find themselves in the line of fire are finding a social sanctuary among their classmates. Students who participate in musical experiences in school are beginning to show signs of extreme tolerance, acceptance, and liberalism across all creeds. Are collegiate and high school students involved in music becoming more socially liberal? Is their musical experience altering their worldviews and political leanings? I plan to prove that involvement in music education, spanning all ensembles from marching to musical theatre, is increasing students' tolerance and acceptance, on both a social and political field. Knowledge and tolerance of race, gender, sexual orientation, gender identity, and religion will be explored. This research will be mostly in the form of blind and random surveys conducted across North Carolina, in school ages from ninth grade to those enrolled in a university or institution of higher learning. Various economic backgrounds will be taken into account to avoid bias on a monetary level. Students surveyed will be currently enrolled or involved in a musical educational experience. Special attention will be paid to statistical significance in these surveys, which will measure students' political affiliation, as well as assess their views on the social aspects of their classrooms or classmates. Interviews will also be filmed and conducted face-to-face with students from several backgrounds and educational levels. Attention will also be given to previous studies which may provide other findings in scholarly musical journals. With these results, it may be shown that students show a higher level of understanding and tolerance towards their classmates; thus, proving that music education can provide a safer and more accepting environment for students in today's hostile culture.

Music Education for Children with Disabilities

Amy C. Elms, author; Judith Jellison, mentor; School of Music, University of Texas, Austin, TX, 2008

As a result of the Individuals with Disabilities Education Act (IDEA), most children with disabilities are now in public schools receiving their education with typical peers. Jellison (2006) had discussed the benefits of a meaningful music education for all children, including those with disabilities. Jellison, Scott, Chappell, and Standridge (2006) also note that inclusion of children with disabilities into regular classrooms with typical children can make the students "'uneasy' about the disabled student's impact on the music performance" (Scott, 49). The purpose of my research with Dr. Jellison is to explore the effects that music education has on children with disabilities (autism) by observing "M", a third-grade student at Gullett Elementary. Observations consist of videotaping the child in his music classroom as he participates in music with typical classmates. In addition, interviews will be conducted with the child, his mother, and his music teacher. The anticipated results will show the music capability of M in this case study. For example, the video observations of M in music class display him using correct vocal tone when singing the patriotic song, "This is My Country." Likewise, he uses correct rhythm when playing class instruments for a Halloween themed song. Finally, he participates in positive social interactions with his peers. For example, he and a typical female classmate successfully participated in a hand clapping game together. In the interview, his mother explained how music is constantly used in M's life. Besides having her son included in music classes at school, she takes her son to recreational music concerts, and has him participate in group violin lessons in order to expand his knowledge of music, desensitize him to loud noises, and encourage the exploration of music with his peers.

The Initial Teaching Experiences of Preservice Music Educators

Dana L. Arbaugh, Devon R. LePore and Christina M. Santoro, authors; Daniel S. Isbell, mentor; Music Education Department, Ithaca College, Ithaca, NY, 2011

The student teaching experience is a critical phase of the occupational socialization of a professional educator. For most music teachers, this student teaching phase begins in the senior year of undergraduate study. The format of music student teaching varies considerably among music teacher preparation programs. Research on the impact of student teaching on the development of future music teachers has shown mixed results. The purpose of this study was to uncover information about the lived experiences of three undergraduate students during the initial four months of their music student teaching experience. The participants in this study are members of a unique junior level student teaching program at a comprehensive college in the northeast United States. In this multiple case self-study, the researchers will collect qualitative data and present their personal experiences during the initial months of this unique junior teaching program. Data sources include self-reflections, cooperating teacher and supervisor feedback, and written self-analysis of videotaped teaching episodes. These data will be coded, salient themes extracted, and findings triangulated to ensure validity. Connections to the university preparation program and the impact on teacher confidence will be explored. Implications for music education and student teaching will also be presented.

Conclusion

Although education is the basis of what occurs at colleges and universities, this discipline is one of the last to embrace undergraduate research fully as an important pedagogy. Perhaps they have been doing it for many years but have not labeled it as such. "When reflecting on their undergraduate research experiences, education students often say that it has provided them with more comprehensive understanding of the field of education and that it has influenced their future teaching career" (Manak & Young, 2014). Go out and discover!

Questions for Discussion

1   What questions might future researchers have?
2   How does music education research reach music teachers?

3   Do you think educational portfolios should be classified as research?
4   What levels of music education research exist?
5   Why is ongoing research important for music educators?
6   Can we really transfer these discovery ideas to students in K-12 classrooms?

References

Harney, K. & Young, G. (2016). Evaluation of two undergraduate research courses in music education: Senior capstone project and teacher work sample. *College Music Symposium*, 56. Retrieved from http://dx.doi.org/10.18177/sym.2016.56.sr.11128 (accessed 23 November 2016).

Manak J. & Young, G. (2014) Incorporating undergraduate research into teacher education: Preparing thoughtful teachers through inquiry-based learning. *CUR Quarterly*, 35(2), 35–38.

Phelps, R. (1983). The first earned doctorate in music education. *The Bulletin of Historical Research in Music Education*, 4(1), 1–6. Retrieved from www.jstor.org/stable/40214639 (accessed 23 November 2016).

15

MUSIC TECHNOLOGY

We are in an electronic technology age now and it's about time we put away the old stuff.

Monica Edwards

Like all tools, modern technology has produced some wonderful moments in music and also some horrors.

Hugh Hopper

The music technology scene is changing so fast it's hard to keep up.

Natasha Bedingfield

Summary

Music technology, by its nature, is an emerging field, and an increasingly popular major for undergraduate students interested in new music and related fields. A variety of topic areas are examined in this chapter, including music in the context of multimedia, the use of particular software and hardware, the science of sound, electronic composition, the use of space, and orchestration for new media. Sample projects and abstracts show students some possibilities for music technology research, followed by questions for discussion.

Introduction

Higher education degrees in music technology are relatively new, but growing in many university music departments and schools. A degree in music technology usually represents a synthesis of traditional musical training and application through new technologies. Students develop skills in areas including music composition and theory, recording, sound synthesis, sound design for film and theater, audio for film/video and multimedia, film scoring, notation and sequencing, orchestration, interdisciplinary collaboration, music business, and instrumental/vocal performance. Working alongside faculty, music technology majors compose original music and collaborate on artistic works and projects with students from across campus. This combination of academic study, creative work, community involvement, and hands-on training produces well-rounded musicians and digital media artists (Bates, 2016).

Music technology faculty and staff often compose new electroacoustic works or get involved in interdisciplinary projects to advance the discipline. Undergraduate researchers in this field can do similar projects, either alongside their professors or on student-directed projects mentored by faculty members.

Music technology students often find a niche or specialty and dig into their chosen interest(s) as they move through the program. For example, some students are quite passionate about the technical aspects of recording or producing either in a live or studio setting. Others are much more composition-oriented. Others still may have a passion for working in film. This much is certain, though: music technology is a field which opens many doors and holds rich potential for a variety of undergraduate research projects for many students.

For the purposes of undergraduate research, it may be helpful to narrow the focus down to a few key aspects of music technology. Multimedia applications, to include interdisciplinary projects, and the marriage of contemporary and traditional methods in music are two rich arenas to explore. Both are consistently relevant and ever-expanding fields within the umbrella of music technology.

In addition to helping with this chapter for his senior capstone course, Logan Henke was one of two music technology students at Montana State University, to have electroacoustic compositions selected for the Electronic Music Midwest Festival in Chicago (2014). His and Jaimie Hensley's compositions were part of the 66 works out of about 250 submissions selected by a jury for performance at the festival. Both works were composed as part of a second-semester freshman music technology course taught by Linda Antas, professor in the MSU School of Music (Salo, 2014).

Multimedia within music technology is most often focused on electroacoustic concert music that is enhanced with other media platforms. Electroacoustic music can be thought of as concert or art music that features electronically created sounds as a major component of the music as a whole. The music may be exclusively electronic or combined with acoustic instruments. So-called concert music is usually created to be the primary focus of the listener, that is to say, the music does not accompany significant social interaction.

FIGURE 15.1 Logan Henke

FIGURE 15.2 Jaimie Hensley

Electroacoustic music can take on a plethora of forms. As mentioned, the electronic portion may appear alone or with an acoustic instrument. In either case, the electronic track is usually—although there are some improvisatory exceptions—prepared and manipulated live via soundboard. Often, electroacoustic music is presented in coordination with a video of some kind, whether it is narrative or not.

However, electroacoustic music may accompany many more mediums of expression. For example, the music may be written alongside choreography of live dancers. Sculpture and similar visual arts may be presented with the music. Instead of video, reaction lights may be used. In the flexible context of the concert hall, the sky is the limit.

Electronic music, and the technology that surrounds it, is a constantly changing landscape. The pace of change due to its association with computer applications is rapid, combined with the creativity of composers thinking up new ways to use these technologies built upon the foundation of traditional art music. The use of surround-sound, other spatial considerations, sounds from nature, or any sound that can be sampled and manipulated to fulfill a composer's intention, are all examples of constantly changing ingredients in electroacoustic music.

An example of an original multimedia application within music is by Montana State University School of Music alumnus, Chris Huvaere. He was fascinated with the physiological phenomena of synesthesia, in which the brain makes strange sensory associations across senses. Huvaere was specifically concerned with chromesthesia, wherein the synesthetic mind has an experience of color upon hearing a certain pitch.

Huvaere set about creating an algorithm which detects the specific musical pitches of a played acoustic instrument. Upon interpreting the pitches, the program he created then matches them to associated colors, and commands a set of lights to change hues appropriately. See abstract below in the sample abstracts.

Another example of effective multimedia work within music technology is the "Black (W)hole" installation, a deeply collaborative work amongst faculty at Montana State University. Created as part of a university campaign to celebrate the work of Albert Einstein, "Black (W)hole" blurs the lines between concert piece and installation. Work on the piece came from physicists, visual artists, and composers associated with Montana State University. Notably, Jason Bolte, School of Music faculty, composed the auditory portion of "Black (W)hole" (Celebrating Einstein, 2014). The piece is fixed media, meaning that both the visual and auditory aspects are prepared and played back at the time of performance. Artistically interpreted visual representations derived from Einstein's work and data concerning black holes is projected on the floor and walls of the space the listener/viewer occupies. An electronic work, developed from and inspired by the gravitational waves a black hole creates, is played in conjunction with the visuals.

These are just a couple of examples of imaginative, original projects that were created within the discipline of music technology.

Traditional and Contemporary Methods

Students of music technology are often tasked with addressing the intersection of traditional and contemporary methods within music composition. For centuries, the method in which composers made music was consistent. When a composer had an idea, pen would have to meet paper to communicate that idea to others. Today, the digital revolution of the late twentieth century has turned that process on its head.

Composers, much like other artists of various disciplines, no longer have to keep their ideas on pen and paper. Composition can, and often does, occur on computer platforms, referred to as digital audio workstations (DAW). DAWs can facilitate everything from synthesis to notation. Audio files and digitally written music can be shown layered onscreen. Musical components such as dynamics, blend, and even spatial placement can be changed on a DAW, even in real time. If this sort of digital notation is an evolution of convenience, then the digital synthesis of both new and recorded sounds is truly a revolution.

Recording arts technologies give composers yet another layer of options. DAWs provide an incredible amount of control and flexibility over the balance and frequency equalization of recorded and synthesized content. In-depth mixing and mastering techniques allow a composer to mold the specific frequency content of sounds. Field recording and sampling also allow a composer to capture found sounds, in the moment. This way, naturally occurring sounds may be captured, perhaps for the first time, and applied musically.

DAWs today give composers, in a word, options. Composers can build sounds from a basic, fundamental waveform, into as complex and rich a texture as they desire. DAWs and hardware such as keyboards and other MIDI-controllers are pre-loaded with sounds, which already provide thousands of options. If those options aren't enough, a composer can build a sound from scratch using analog hardware and coding applications. Therefore, the sonic palette that is available to composers today is vast and truly limitless.

With such a massive amount of sonic options available to composers today, a question then arises. What is the use in returning to traditional instrumentation and compositional methods? Although this question alone can prompt constant discussion, the present compositional landscape is clear. Composers continue to use traditional instrumentation and textures, even alongside electronically created music.

Whereas some may observe a divide growing between these two compositional realms, some composers embrace the two. An outstanding example is Mason Bates, an American composer born in 1977. Bates' website markets him as a composer of both "classical" and "electronica" music. Bates, a composer who has been in residence with such ensembles as the Chicago Symphony Orchestra, is well-known for blending the orchestra with electronic music. He has a long catalog of works which blend the two worlds effectively. Bates' music is a good starting point for exploring the ways in which composers come to terms with the techniques available today (Bates, 2016).

Possible Topics

- Create a real-time algorithmic method of identifying musical features;
- analyze adaptive music and leitmotifs in video games;
- use spectromorphology for visual examination of selected new music;
- discover how technology in DIY venues shaped popular music;
- examine streaming, a major shift in the music industry;
- choir with electronics: a medium for compositional exploration;
- examine how copyright laws apply to new technologies and content;
- digital measurements of the timbral differences in guitar tonewoods;
- in defense of noise: an exploration of contemporary noise music;
- from eye to ear: the connections between visual art and music;
- explore how music technology can be used to enhance music performance;
- compose and perform using various technologies;
- an original arrangement of an acoustic composition done electronically;
- explore alternate intonation (this could be researching this field, composing using microtones, etc.);
- use music technology to help musicians improve their intonation;
- find different environments in which to use music technologies;

- mix acoustic sounds from nature with traditional instruments;
- measure acoustic properties of different spaces;
- research and/or produce music sample libraries;
- explore how much the quality of a tuner affects the resulting sound (can compare several instruments).

Sample Abstracts Submitted to NCUR

www.cur.org/conferences_and_events/student_events/ncur/archive/

An Examination of the Attitudes towards Online Music Sharing and Downloading

Alex Durante, Nicholas Pepe, Andrew Herschman, and Derek Little, authors; Karen Becker, mentor; Department of Marketing, The College of New Jersey, Ewing, NJ, 2012

The music industry faces a crisis. As of 2009, 95 percent of online music downloads are illegal. Revenues for artists and record companies are diminishing substantially. Unfortunately, this trend is not likely to recede, as teenagers continue to value music as a form of entertainment that is simply not worth paying for. Confronted with teenagers' expectations that music should be free, the music industry must concentrate on curbing illegal downloading behavior. This paper examines the attitudes towards the behavior expressed by people who illegally download music. When respondents were prompted with two illegal music downloading scenarios, both involving fictitious students who used file sharing programs, results indicated that the respondents did not perceive online music sharing as theft, confirming previous research. Consequently, this study shows that these people do not experience guilt when engaging in this behavior. The results also show that respondents were unsure about whether there should be consequences for illegal music downloading. This uncertainty seems to suggest that people who illegally download music believe there should be consequences but would not want to be punished for engaging in such behavior. Finally, when people choose not to illegally download music, they do so because of self-enhancing motives. That is, people avoid illegal music downloading not as a result of concern for the artists or record companies, but due to a fear of computer infections and viruses. The results reveal that increasing the self-enhancing benefits of not illegally downloading music is essential to deterring this behavior.

A Breath from an Electronic World: Experiments in Musical Expression Using a Midi Wind Controller

Matthew Ahrens, author; James Bohn, mentor; Department of Music, Bridgewater State University, Bridgewater, MA, 2011

Unlike their keyboard and percussion counterparts, the potential of the wind controller is still a largely unexplored venture. From the introduction of the Lyricon in the 1970s, the potential of the wind controller has remained widely unnoticed. This project delved into the history of wind controllers, explained how they communicate with sound modules and software via the midi language, and compared them to familiar acoustic musical instruments—such as saxophone— and electronic musical instruments—such as the electronic keyboard. The musical potential of the midi wind controller was then assessed by its expressive ability and variety of human input parameters. In conducting the technical and historical research on the wind controller, two main issues became apparent. The first issue is that wind synthesists tend to limit themselves to using the controller to emulate modern, acoustic instrument sounds. Similarly, the second issue is that there are few musical works specifically composed to utilize the abilities unique to the wind controller; wind controllers are most commonly being used to play jazz, single-line melody parts typically reserved for saxophone. In order to address these issues, several patches—controllable sound banks—were created to test the capabilities of the wind controller beyond emulation. The wind controller experimented with for this project was the Akai Electronic Wind Instrument 4000s. Traditional sounds were recorded and programmed so that they could be performed using the wind controller in ways not humanly possible acoustically in real time. For example, steel string, acoustic guitar, and nylon string, acoustic guitar were sampled and modeled for use with Roland Fantom-XR sound module. The wind controller was then programmed to transition between the timbres at will, even during sustain. Materials such as ice and concrete, which would be impractical for the construction of modern, concert instruments, were made into simple instruments, recorded and modeled, and then programmed to be manipulated by the wind controller. Other tonal colors were also explored. In order to showcase the utility of these new patches, musical works were composed. These works showcase the wind controller's ability as a melodic, rhythmic, and harmonic instrument. They explore the underemphasized aspects of the wind controller and serve as etudes for future wind synthesists to study. This project is made in the hope to be representative of the wind controller community. It aims to increase awareness of the potential of wind controllers as a tool of musical expression. Lastly, this project is being presented in the hopes that the research conducted, the patches created for use with wind controller, and the score and recordings of the musical works composed will aid the composers, wind synthesists, and music programmers of today.

Replicating the Sound of a Stradivarius Violin with 3D Printing

Steven Britt, author; Paula Bobrowski, mentor; Department of Music, Auburn University, Auburn, AL, 2016

Materials have a profound effect on the characteristics of musical instruments. To illustrate, most wind instruments are classified according to sound-producing material: woodwind or brass. Yet materials determine even more subtle characteristics. The timbre of a guitar is determined by the species of wood used. All are guitars, but a different material will subtly change the sound. In the past, the master of musical materials was Italian luthier Antonio Stradivari. Scientists seek to replicate the beautiful, powerful sound Stradivari's instruments provided but have not yet succeeded. "Can the advantages of 3D printing and digital design produce a 3D printed violin that matches the sound of a Stradivari violin?" New research has suggested that Stradivari's secret was his materials: the chemical composition of Stradivari's violins and cellos differ vastly from the wood of modern violins. Reproducing the material Stradivari used may lead to replicating his violins' sound. While some researchers look to replicate instruments of the past, others look to advance instrument design. A French team has developed the 3D-Varius, a 3D-printed electric violin. Among the many advantages 3D printing provides is the ability to produce an instrument made from one solid piece of material. Frequencies can now propagate throughout the instrument, producing both a smooth sound and greater predictability for acoustical response. Because of the predictability, a Stradivari violin might be easier reproduced by 3D printing rather than woodworking. Each separate piece of a violin has a different resonate frequency thus producing complex interactions making it difficult to predict. This research aims to determine if the advantages of 3D printing are able to rival the hand of a master craftsman in instrument fabrication.

Two Abstracts from Montana (Campus Presentations)

The Art of Sound

Sarah Fugman, author; Richard Hughes, mentor; University of Montana, Missoula, MT, 2016

I have assembled a collection of my sonic art projects and combined them into a sound trailer. The piece is showcasing my abilities as a sound artist and what I have learned and created in the media arts program. My goal as a sonic artist is to become a sound designer for a film production company. The first piece is a sonic portrait that paints an audio picture of my internal process of interacting with my favorite films, which have had a huge impact on my life. The challenge was to create a sound piece that described this without any visuals to rely on. The second piece is from my first semester at the University of Montana. I chose a music video by the "Lonely Island," and re-articulated the sonic environment by creating a new and unique sonic pallet. Using Adobe Premiere Pro video editing software I re-edited the visuals, and using Logic Pro 9 audio software, I created the final audio mix which included dialogue, ambient sound, foley, and effects. The third piece expanded my abilities by introducing a programming language into the creation of sonic art. Programming allows me to create real time interactive sonic art experiences. This project challenged me to think differently about sound and opened up a new world of sonic possibilities. The last piece is part of a project I have been working on for a while. Similar to my second piece, I removed all the sound from the music video "I bet my Life" by Imagine Dragons and re-articulated the sonic environment. With so many projects to create and learn from, I continue to explore the numerous possibilities in sound advancements from designing a sound studio to exploring different kinds of audio software programs.

Real-Time Algorithm for Identifying Messiaen's Color Modes

Chris Huvaere, author; Laurel Yost, mentor; School of Music, Montana State University, Bozeman, MT, 2015

We consider a real-time algorithm for identifying Messiaen's color modes in real-time performances of his works. Messiaen's color modes are a subset of his modes of limited transposition. These modes have well-documented color associations within Messiaen's writings and correlate strongly with his synesthesia. We discuss several of the complexities associated with mode identification in general and their implications on real-time analysis of Messiaen's works. The algorithm under consideration extracts a 12-dimensional chroma vector describing the note content from recent pitch events occurring in an incoming audio signal. This vector is then used to calculate a nearest-neighbor from the collection of Messiaen's color modes.

Questions for Discussion

1   How has technology changed our musical perception?
2   Where will music technology be in the future?
3   How common will/has music technology become?
4   Will electronic music eventually replace live music?
5   Why does this sort of music really only occur in an academic setting?
6   How can the use of space be used to create aesthetic experiences?
7   Should we blend traditional music with electronic music? Why or why not?

References

Bates, M. (2016). MasonBates.com. Retrieved from www.masonbates.com/ (accessed 16 December 2016).

Celebrating Einstein. (2014). Celebrating Einstein. Retrieved from http://blackwhole. montana.edu/index.htm (accessed 6 December 2016).

Montana State University School of Music, Music Technology. (n.d.). Retrieved from www.montana.edu/music/musictech/ (accessed 1 December 2016).

Salo, W. (2014). Music technology students' works selected to national festival. Montana State University. Retrieved from www.montana.edu/news/12747/music-technology-students-works-selected-to-national-festival (accessed 1 December 2016).

16
MUSIC THERAPY

Simply put, music can heal people.

Senator Harry Reid

Music is therapy. Music moves people. It connects people, in ways no other medium can. It pulls heartstrings; it acts as medicine.

Macklemore

Music therapy, to me, is music performance without the ego. It's not about entertainment as much as it's about empathizing. If you can use music to slip past the pain and gather insight into the workings of someone else's mind, you can begin to fix a problem.

Jodi Picoult, *Sing You Home*

Summary

Music therapy has been a growing area of interest for many college music majors recently, and it provides a context for a variety of student research projects. Parallels with art therapy and dance therapy have been drawn, and there are a variety of different medical reasons that health professionals recommend music therapy as part of treatment regimens. As the baby boom generation becomes the elderly, there has been an increased demand for music therapy, not only for its healing potential, but also as prevention. Project ideas will be outlined and sample abstracts will give students an idea of the scope of possible projects. Students do not have to be music therapy majors to explore projects in this area. Many students including majors from several other fields have been interested in and have completed rewarding research projects.

Introduction

Formally, music therapy involves working with a trained music therapist, either individually or in a group setting, who uses music for healing purposes or for general health and prevention (Bumanis, 2014). For example, even undergraduate research studies have shown that Alzheimer's patients who listen to music that they enjoyed in their younger years become more lucid, even temporarily. On a less formal level, music can be beneficial by just having someone playing music in the social room of a nursing home, for personal benefit and/or the benefit of the listeners.

Recently opened in Toronto, Canada, the Dotsa Bitove Wellness Center is a part of the University Health Network (UHN) and provides dementia patients with opportunities to play and listen to music, and participate in visual art forms among other art practices. This author (Young) attended the opening of the center with Dr. Jocelyn Charles and heard many testimonials from medical professionals who had personal experience reducing prescriptions thanks to musical involvement by patients. Many optimistically predicted that this center, modeled on a similar one in Florida, would benefit dementia patients tremendously (Dotsa Bitove Wellness Academy, 2013).

MSU senior Miranda LeBrun chose to focus on this chapter due to a personal circumstance. While other students had previous experience and prior knowledge of neuroscience, how the brain works with music and what parts of the brain are used when listening to/playing music, her inspiration comes from her mother. Recently, her mother was in a rather unique and life-changing accident; sadly, not in a good way. Without going into the details of the accident, she now has a traumatic brain injury (TBI), difficulty using one of her arms, a broken septum, and a majority of her teeth have nerve damage (basically, they are dead because of the damage and lack of blood flow). She took piano lessons for approximately 13 years when she was younger and has always wanted a piano in her house. It took a TBI to make it happen, but they finally have a piano, and she is able to play. Miranda has been hopeful that ever since the accident and piano purchase that her mother would regain many functions such as her short-term memory, control of emotions, and concentration to name a few. Without music, the recovery process could take much longer. Her muscle memory has come back rather quickly but it is difficult to focus on the notes, especially in extreme ranges (those darn ledger lines!), and she often forgets if she has already played a repeated section. Although she has made great progress so far, her bad habit of not counting the beats while she plays has followed her from childhood, and it makes it difficult to play duets with her. Miranda wanted to work on this chapter to better understand what her mother was going through and to see if she could help her through music. It is a slow recovery process, but Miranda believes she is getting better and that the piano is one of her best recovery tools.

There is an important distinction between non-clinical music therapy and professional music therapy done by a licensed practitioner. The following lists serve to clarify that distinction.

Non-clinical music therapy:

- player pianos in building's lobby;
- musical performances at hospitals and schools;
- students volunteering to perform at nursing homes;
- nurses playing background music for patients;
- people with degenerative diseases listening to favorite songs of the past.

Licensed music therapists treating patients in a formal setting to:

- regain speech after traumatic brain injuries;
- lessen the effects of dementia;
- reduce asthma episodes;
- reducing pain in general for hospitalized patients;
- improving communication of children diagnosed with autism;
- work with premature infants to improve sleep patterns and increase weight gain;
- regaining muscle control for those diagnosed with Parkinson's disease.

Music used for healing purposes dates back to ancient times. In the Western world however, it began most noticeably during the World War eras. The National Association for Music Therapy founded was in 1950 and was most utilized by veterans. Since this time, an increasing interest in music therapy as a profession has emerged. As of November 2016, there were 73 accredited schools offering bachelor degrees, 38 schools offering master's degrees, and 8 that offer doctoral degrees. More information about music therapy organizations can be found in Chapter 19, Online Resources.

Music and Memory

Does music help with memory? In therapy sessions, music has been successful with helping people remember things from their past. Music seems to be a transportation device used to take people of any age to a different time and place. Memories of what specific things people were doing at that moment often comes back to them, along with the associated emotion.

Physical, Mental, and Emotional Healing

Recent research shows that patients with a variety of medical conditions such as autism, depression, dementia, and insomnia can benefit from music if the right type of music is used appropriately. "People who have autism spectrum disorders often show a heightened interest and response to music. This may aid in the teaching of verbal and nonverbal communication skills and in establishing normal developmental processes" (Ulbricht, 2013).

Music and the Brain

There are many questions that are currently being examined with the assistance of functional magnetic resonance imaging (FMRI). What happens to your brain when you listen to music? What happens when you actively participate in music? What parts of the brain are in use? How will this help with healing and medical advances? Upon completion of the interdisciplinary seminar relevant to this topic, discussed in Chapter 11 of this book, one of the professors (Miller) used a program called Mindwave Manager to observe brain wave activity while one of the students improvised jazz on the saxophone. This was cutting edge research at the time and they were able to do it thanks to emerging technology.

Possible Topics

- Examine studies that link music therapy with speech therapy;
- investigate effects of music on patients in a coma, interview staff that take care of them (the medical personnel);
- music and memory: survey staff and family members to find out how effective musical interventions are with dementia patients;
- compare silent meditation and meditations accompanied by music;
- survey music majors to see what musical components are most effective for healing;
- review recent literature on music and memory;
- arrange a medley of famous old tunes designed to be therapeutic for a certain age group;
- compose an original piece for meditation;
- interview music therapists to find out what they like most and least about their job, with examples;
- what is the difference between live music and recorded music in therapy settings;
- singing bowls and their use in therapy;
- examine the use of mindfulness in music therapy settings;
- effects on different ages (young vs. old)—preventative measures;

- interview music therapists and musicians that play in the hospitals;
- combining music with other things like the smells and the colors of the room;
- find a medical condition that is used for music therapy (lots of research out there on Alzheimer's) and figure out how it affects the brain and what the success rates are. What conditions haven't been tried?
- research how the Mozart Effect impacts people who have mental illness;
- investigate any adverse effects that music therapy has had on patients;
- music therapy and palliative care—survey of the attitudes of patients, staff, and medical personnel concerning the efficacy of music therapy in clinics.

Sample Undergraduate Abstracts

Genre Specificity of Extra-task Stimulation on Mathematics Performance in Children with ADHD (Campus Presentation)

Andrew Major, author; John Miller, mentor; Montana State University; Bozeman, MT, 2013

This study evaluated the dependence of musical genre of extra-task auditory stimulation on the arithmetic performance of children diagnosed with attention deficit hyperactivity disorder (ADHD). Two boys with ADHD worked on a mathematics task after various music stimulations and during the same music stimulations. Most music stimulation enhanced mathematical performance for both subjects, with the hip-hop rap genre being an exception, as it resulted in performance below the control in silence. Almost no variation in accuracy was observed for either subject; instead the number of problems attempted was most impacted. A noticeable dependence on musical genre as well as the subject's rating of each genre's pleasantness was found for the number of problems attempted by Subject 1. For the Subject 2, however, there was less discrimination between genres but still a general increase in performance with music stimulation. There was some division between the results of music stimulation which occurred before versus during the task as stimulation during the task had a more marked impact. The facilitative effects of music stimulation on the mathematical performance of the children with ADHD provide support for the optimal stimulation theory developed by Zentall (1975) which posits that children with ADHD demonstrate high levels of activity when faced with a situation of low arousal. Music stimulation can serve as a stimulant that raises arousal, in turn helping focus and perform the intended task.

Music Living Those Songs Again: Music for Memory Care (Campus Conference)

Keeli Telleen, capstone project; Gregory Young, mentor; Montana State University School of Music; Bozman, MT, 2016

To shed light on the relationship between music, memory, and emotion, particularly in elderly adults with memory deficiencies, I plan to investigate the effects of music on memory care residents. Research by Simmons-Stern, Budson, and Ally (2010) suggests music can enhance memory in Alzheimer's patients. El Haj, Fasotti, and Allain (2012) discuss how listening to preferred music evokes memories that are more specific and have more emotional content than when individuals try to retrieve memories in silence. Further, a large body of research supports music listening as an effective form of therapy for individuals with various forms of dementia. My goal is to build upon these findings using qualitative methods. I will assist in the Music and Memory program at Spring Creek Inn Memory Care Center, where custom playlists are gathered with music from residents' youth to tap into memory, aid in therapy, and improve cognition. Through interactions and observations, I will study the effects of music on their memory and behavior. Following up with individual interviews of family members and caretakers, I intend to generate new insights and disseminate ideas for family involvement with loved ones who suffer memory loss.

Sample Abstracts Submitted to NCUR

www.cur.org/conferences_and_events/student_events/ncur/archive/

Clinical Applications for Percussion Techniques

Hana J. Dehtiar, Megan Hoffman, and Jessica Mumford authors; Lee, Anna Rasar, mentor; Music and Theatre Arts, University of Wisconsin-Eau Claire, Eau Claire, WI, 2008

This session integrates ethnic as well as clinical diversity with therapeutic applications for percussion techniques and provides an innovative model in that it is taught one day weekly in the classroom and one day weekly in the clinical setting. Students gain experience with percussion applications for a variety of populations including: autism spectrum disorder; dementia; reactive attachment disorder; communication disorders; Parkinson's disease; Huntington's disease; learning disabilities; ADD/ADHD; other cognitive disabilities; and stroke. On the days that the course meets in the community settings it is held at the juvenile detention center, the home of a young Asian woman with a developmental disability and ADHD, and on a dementia unit at a nursing home, with students rotating through these three populations across the semester. Goals range from attention focus, impulse control, mood redirection, and anger management to improvement of gait, decrease in stuttering, improvement in cross-lateral movement and visual field cuts, and executive function training. The instruments and musical structures in the African, Middle Eastern, Native American, and Asian cultures are studied. Creation of a notebook with session plans and critiques for each session as well as a master discography of musical resources coded to represent the various areas of diversity is required. As a result of the success of the pilot class, the course is now a required course in the curriculum. The series of research grants represented by this presentation allowed for the development of content for this course as well as for pilot teaching and assessment of it. Results of the research have been presented at two regional and two national music therapy conferences and are in the process of being posted on a new website.

The Effects of Music Therapy on Alzheimer's Disease Patients: The Best Is Yet to Come

Amanda L. Scott, author; Cheryl Anagnopoulos, mentor; Department of Psychology, Black Hills State University, Spearfish, SD, 2008

Alzheimer's Disease is the most prevalent form of dementia in elderly people, currently affecting about 4.5 million Americans (ADEAR, 2006). This population's size clearly displays the need for research into alternative therapies such as music therapy. There is a great deal of successful research on the application of music therapy for problematic behaviors in Alzheimer's patients, such as Ledger and Baker's 2006 study. However, I have not found published research on the subject of generational music and its effects on the behavior of Alzheimer's patients. I will conduct a study on the effect of specific generational music on Alzheimer's patient's behavior. My study involves conducting typical music therapy sessions with two groups of Alzheimer's patients, including eight participants per group. The control group will have group music therapy with simple folk songs. The test group will have group music therapy with specifically chosen songs from their young adulthood years. Sessions will be conducted three times per week for six weeks. Behavior testing will be conducted via the Cohen-Mansfield Agitation Inventory form (Cohen-Mansfield, Marx & Rosenthal, 1989). The behavior observation of each participant in both groups is conducted and reported by facility staff. I will conduct the music therapy group sessions as well as interview facility staff about each participant's behavior. I expect to find that the test group benefits significantly from generational music therapy sessions and that the control group benefits somewhat from therapy sessions. The benefits from music therapy will be determined through agitation behaviors decreasing.

The Effects of Music on Exercise

Taylor Adams, author; Michael Olpin, mentor; College of Education, Weber State University, Ogden, UT, 2016

Research concerning the positive effects music has on exercise is prevalent and continues to be evaluated. Studies show that by adding music to a workout, the individual can experience improved mood state, increased arousal, and a reduced feeling of fatigue. Background music has been shown to lower perceived exertion rate by about 10 percent, therefore, enhancing endurance. Overall, music increases motivation or the rate of perceived exertion and tends to lower stress levels. With this information, it is obvious; there is a connection between music and exercise. This study focused primarily on people's perceptions of how music affects their workout as well as behaviors regarding the frequency of physical activity and the use of music. Initially we hypothesized that those who frequently listen to music during their workout would feel strongly about its positive effects while those who rarely listen to music during their workout would disagree. A survey was given to 102 volunteer students at Weber State University. Among the results we found that 57 percent of those surveyed said that they always or frequently listened to music during their workout. Among those surveyed, 68 percent either agreed or strongly agreed that music reduced fatigue, 85 percent believed music increased motivation, and 69 percent felt a decrease in stress levels when incorporating music into their workout. Our findings suggest that overall the participants surveyed felt that music positively affected their workout.

Conclusion

Music therapy is becoming a prominent field of study and method of healing. Though we have no way of knowing what the future may hold, advances in neuroscience research combined with important technologies such as the FMRI, appear positive. Music has aided people of all ages with a variety of conditions and greatly improved the lives of many families. The medical profession is becoming increasingly aware of the benefits of music therapy, as well as art therapy, and can actually reduce the number and dosages of medicines that patients need for certain conditions. This subject holds promise for both qualitative and quantitative undergraduate research.

Questions for Discussion

1 What medical advances are changing music therapy?
2 What is the history of music therapy?
3 How can we predict the future of music therapy?
4 What are the enrollment trends in university music therapy programs?
5 Why do some music programs not include music therapy in their degree programs?
6 What are the statistics on the different conditions treated with music therapy?

References

Bumanis, A. (2014). Setting the record straight: what music therapy is and what it is NOT American Music Therapy Association. Retrieved from www.musictherapy.org/amta_press_release_on_music_therapy_-_jan_2014/ (accessed 3 January 2017).
Dotsa Bitove Wellness Academy. (2013). Speech at the Academy's opening ceremony.
Ulbricht, C. (2013). Music therapy for health and wellness. Retrieved from www.psychologytoday.com/blog/natural-standard/201306/music-therapy-health-and-wellness (accessed 30 November 2016).

17

ETHNOMUSICOLOGY, CULTURE, AND POPULAR MUSIC

All music is structurally, as well as functionally, 'folk' music in the sense that music cannot be transmitted or have meaning without associations between people.

John Blacking, *How Musical is Man?*

Music does bring people together. It allows us to experience the same emotions. People everywhere are the same in heart and spirit. No matter what language we speak, what color we are, the form of our politics or the expression of our love and our faith, music proves: We are the same.

John Denver

Summary

Every known human society has music—but are those sounds that they make over in that country really "music?" one might ask. A people is reflected in their music. And now, with the aid of technology, the music of the world are available to be heard. Now more than ever, we can close the musical gap between cultures and between nations. When music meets anthropology, sociology, language and more, we get ethnomusicology. This chapter investigates what music is, discusses the relationships between various kinds of music and the peoples that belong with them, and outlines the research process of fieldwork with its inherent adventures and issues. Included are suggestions for capstone topics, sample abstracts of completed projects, and questions for discussion.

Music and Ethnomusicology

What is music? Most of us might be hard-pressed to come up with a satisfying and comprehensive answer to this question. Bruno Nettl, the famous ethnomusicologist, notes in his book, *The Study of Ethnomusicology*, this simple definition found in *Webster's Intermediate Dictionary*: music is "the art of combining tones so that they are pleasing, expressive, or intelligible" (Nettl, 1983, p. 18). But do societies the world over claim a similar definition? Each people's music, worthy of study and appreciation, must be, and possibly can only be, understood as a part of its people.

> If we wish to identify what it is that determines the nature of a particular music, we should look first to the general character of its culture and particularly the types of relationships among people within its society.
>
> (Nettl, 2003, p. 20)

Ethnomusicology is often viewed as a combination of musicology and anthropology, and according to Montana State University professor David Charles, "musicology has been influenced by ethnomusicology insofar as musicologists are now placing more emphasis on a given tradition's sociocultural context" (Charles, 2017).

Music and Society

History reveals the rich melting pot of sounds that occurs over time at the hands of the schooled and unschooled, the East and the West, the cultured and the archaic. Be inspired to discover the sound palates of your own backyard. Some historical examples might shed light on the subject and inspire some interesting project ideas. Bartok synthesized his musical roots in the classical tradition with the voices of Eastern European peasants to develop his own compositional voice. The migratory climate of post-Civil War America heard Delta Blues music at the shipping ports of New Orleans, along with the slave spirituals of the southern plantations, the rhythms of the Caribbean, and the operatic classics of Western Europe. Believing to be led by the divine, Native American folk singers discovered spirit songs through dreams and coming of age journeys.

A Local Lens for Ethnomusicology

Which cultures are represented around you? Consider conducting interviews and surveys with international exchange students at your university. Which musical events are showcased near you? Visit, observe, and record the happenings at India Culture Night. Which venues serve as art or music hubs?

Find a coffee shop or bar or art gallery that partners with local musicians and investigate its impact in the community. What subgenre social groups in your area associate themselves with a particular music? Meet and interview kids at the skate park and research their playlists. Perhaps a faculty member is from a distant musical heritage, or maybe you have encountered foreign music and/ or unusual instruments while studying abroad. Many composers have been inspired to introduce international aspects into their compositions by their own foreign travel. Examples abound, such as "Brasileira" from *Scaramouche* by Darius Milhaud; the Hungarian Dances by Johannes Brahms; "Tambourin Chinois" by Fritz Kreisler; and many others.

Research Process

Field Work

How does one conduct research of a society's music? This process is referred to as fieldwork. After preliminary research of the particular music—and that music's society—fieldwork requires the researcher to go to the venue, event, society; and then to observe, interview, record; and finally to report back. The goal as the participant is cultural immersion, and becoming an active observer— you are in the audience, experiencing the music as the people of that culture experience it. Take detailed notes as the observer, interview the players, and if possible, record the music.

Fieldwork research may be conducted anywhere at any kind of event for any kind of music. Interest in the ways in which music plays a role in the ritual of a religious ceremony may lead a fieldworker to attend said kind of service, participating as much as possible, interviewing other participators, and recording the experience through note-taking and audio/visual technology. Participating as an audience member of a concert, speaking with the group's tour fans, and researching the fan base all constitute as fieldwork.

Issues

Interpretation of the world around us will inevitably be colored by our position as observers. Coming from our various cultures and contexts, the task of comprehending another culture's sound and worldview is a difficult one. This tension between objectivity and bias from our own music is commonly referred to as "cultural relativism." True objectivity is simply unattainable, however fieldworkers must interact as directly as possible with a culture to begin to understand the peoples that they are studying. Library collections of ethnomusicological findings today exist in large part because of the insiders from societies the world over who have undertaken the work of making their sounds and ways known to outsiders. Recordings, video, and literature abound for us to begin the ear-opening adventure of hearing, and hopefully learning to love, the music of the world. What music did you grow up hearing? Through what kind of auditory framework do you hear music from other cultures? How does one begin to rebuild, or add on to, that framework?

Music Appreciation

Unfortunately, the inherently egocentric nature that we detect within ourselves marks us as societies as well. Perhaps particularly in Western culture, we have tended to call our way the best way, perhaps the only way. If other music does not sound very similar to ours, is it actually music? Again according to Nettl's observations, we in the West tend to see music as inherently good, and therefore it ought to be enjoyable. This enjoyableness is valuable to us, and says something of what we perceive the purpose of music to be. There are many other purposes for music in many other cultures, and some even view music as sinful. Through the study of ethnomusicology, or simply studying the music of other cultures, we can learn a lot about other cultures and societies and discover useful musical components that can enhance our compositions. See the example of Anthony Gaglia's composition, "Impressions of Haiti" and subsequent presentation at the World Congress on Undergraduate Research in Qatar, in Chapter 10 of this book.

Possible Topics

- Interview international students who are taking music theory in the United States and ask them how they perceive the differences between Western classical music and the music of their culture;
- explore how studying another country's culture can inform the study of the music that country produces;
- bring home an instrument from a study abroad trip that is not common in your own environment and learn to play it as you research music written for it;
- compare the musical rhythms of another culture with Western classical rhythms;
- analyze the ways in which a given country's music is incorporated into music by American composers;
- interview regional composers about international influences in their music;
- study the components of the gamelans of Asia, and their histories;
- study the governmental support for traditional music in various countries, as the younger generations gravitate toward Western music;
- research governmental censure and its effect on the music of certain composers;
- find out how immigrant composers' music changed when they immigrated;

- analyze Western influences into popular music in Asia;
- study the folk influences in the music of Stravinsky;
- examine what makes Spanish music sound Spanish, and how those elements migrate to other cultures.

Sample Abstracts Submitted to NCUR

www.cur.org/conferences_and_events/student_events/ncur/archive/

Pungmulnori *and Effective Community "Re-Making"*

Nikolas C. Nadeau, author; Michael Opitz, mentor; Department of English, College of St. Benedict/St. John's University, Collegeville, MN, 2008

Since its arrival to the U.S. in 1985, the Korean traditional percussion form known as *pungmulnori* has blossomed as a ubiquitous and dynamic force in Korean American communities. Involving four instruments and a plethora of rhythms and dance movements, *pungmulnori* has helped Korean American communities conduct "the process of defining and creating new identities, be they individual, generational, Korean, Korean American or otherwise" (Kwon, 2001). My research seeks to determine how *pungmulnori* has helped re-define and re-create (or together, "re-make") the Korean American community in the Minneapolis-St. Paul (Twin Cities) area. Based on textual and interview-based research, I will trace *pungmulnori*'s emergence in the U.S. and gather testimonial evidence to its function as an intracommunity mortar in the Twin Cities. Textual evidence will include scholarly articles by Jennifer L. Bussell (1997) and Donna Lee Kwon (2001), while testimonial evidence will derive from interviews of members of Shinparam, a Twin Cities-based *pungmulnori* troupe, including Korean nationals (Korean citizens residing in the U.S.), Korean Americans (adopted and non-adopted Koreans with U.S. citizenship), Caucasian adoptive parents, and other Caucasian group members who profess an interest in Korean culture. In my presentation I will argue that *pungmulnori* models successful community "re-making" by cultivating attentive listening, active response, and what I call "interdependence awareness." In addition to instilling a unifying and relational spirit in *pungmulnori* group members, this modeling also invites members of other cultural communities to engage in dialogue and cooperative community activism. I will conclude the presentation by performing a traditional solo piece entitled "Sol-janngo" to demonstrate *pungmulnori*'s holistic and "re-creative" spirit.

Music Capture and Release: Exploring Photography, Videography, Audio Production, and the Implications of Ethnomusicology Fieldwork in the Twenty-First Century

Will Baxley, author; Janet Haavisto, faculty mentor; Jacksonville University, Jacksonville, FL, 2015

Ethnomusicology is the systemic study of music cultures and the impact of these musics on humanity. Inherently, to observe the role of music, one must attempt to objectively witness or experience people and the way music affects them. This "observing" frequently takes place in some manner of "fieldwork." Though the label of "ethnomusicology" is not old, heretofore the general practices of studying different music cultures have remained similar (if not contiguous) throughout history. As technology advanced and the world became more globalized in the twentieth century, fieldwork also began to evolve. Now even more so, fieldwork in the twenty-first century changes so quickly that authorities in the field can scarcely assert a common practice in publication before it becomes obsolete. As was true in centuries past, fieldwork practices rely greatly on the funding, and subsequently the equipment, available to the researcher. This thesis seeks to utilize practices used in a specific example of an ethnomusicology fieldwork re-study in Kenya to discuss plausible transcendent applications of technology to a wide variety of field research budgets. By focusing on certain parameters and priorities involved in the fieldwork (and its subsequent publications) it is possible to glean more general concepts that have withstood time and can continue to help in the understanding of practical research in the field. The topics of photography, videography, and audio production are integral to the current model of field research. This thesis touches on each at a conceptual level that both defines practices at this specific moment in technological history while also discussing each at an abstract level that will allow the information to bleed through to future generations of methodology. Naturally, as the methods of fieldwork change, the implicit effects fieldwork can have on a culture or community also change. The conclusion of this thesis attempts to weigh the consequences of the philosophical and ethical concerns posed with present-day fieldwork.

Pop Will Erase Itself: Music Criticism and Culture after the Digital Turn

Thomas Lawson, author; Aaron M. McKain, mentor; English Department, Hamline University, Saint Paul, MN, 2015

If 1967 had the Beatles and 1977 had punk, did the 2000s offer an identifiable, novel sound or counterculture? This is the question that has agitated rock critics since the end of the 00s. For the first time since rock's conception, popular music lacked a cultural touchstone. What catalyzed the 2000s' facelessness? Did iPods and online radio make music too available and our listening disengaged? Or, as rock journalist Simon Reynolds has argued, were the 2000s simply nostalgic and stylistically exhausted? Arguing against the assumption that contemporary pop music is aesthetically drained, I want to argue that today's listener's interpretive strategies have changed through digital technology, which facilitates our untrammeled access to music's recorded history. I contend that the 2000s' facelessness is best explained not as the rise of postmodern pastiche, but the listener's hyperawareness of popular music's history. To unsettle Reynolds' claims regarding music's stylistic stasis, my presentation turns to electroacoustic improvisation, or EAI, a contemporary genre of experimental music. In contrast to popular music, EAI's aesthetic forces listeners to expend an ordinate amount of time and attention while listening to nearly silent performances. This presentation unpacks EAI's aesthetic, which privileges improvisation, silence, and non-musical instruments over melodicism, to articulate how the hyperaware listener recognizes and interprets popular music's stylistics. In conjunction with the explication of EAI's aesthetic, I build upon Barry Brummett's rhetorical model and the Deleuzo-Guattarian concept of the refrain to delineate how print media could produce the semblance of aesthetic cohesion and novelty. Moreover, by considering today's hyperaware listener, I argue that the history of recorded music and the digital interface are erasing the possibility of popular culture and aesthetic cohesion. In this way, I diagnose music criticism and cultural participation today while describing their precarious future.

The Role of the Avant Garde Coffeehouse in the Folk/Blues Revival

Brian Burke, author; John Stropes, mentor; Music Department, University of Wisconsin-Milwaukee, Milwaukee, WI, 2012

The Avant Garde Coffeehouse was a Milwaukee music club which, from 1962–1968, was the locus of the folk/blues revival in Wisconsin. There were places like this in other geographic areas, but, in Wisconsin, none as important as the Avant Garde. It presented local performers and national touring artists, poetry readings, and art films. Patrons regarded the music with the same seriousness and respect given to classical music. It was a classroom. You went there to learn. You could actually sit down and have a conversation with these performers. Without the Avant Garde, there would have been no centrality for these older traditions or the recasting of these traditions by revivalists. Within this was an embedded cultural desire for something else. It was not freezing a moment in time, it was thawing a moment in time. The origins of the singer/songwriter movement come out radically from younger players modeling themselves after older ones, but advancing with hip originality of their own. As the emphasis shifted toward originality, the stage was set for a more artful approach to instrumental guitar music. Much has been written about music clubs like this in other geographic areas, but the role of the Avant Garde Coffeehouse in the folk/blues revival has been largely unrecognized. This project brings together information on the life and legacy of the Avant Garde Coffeehouse and the history of the building that it occupied. We began by interviewing the dramatis personae, discovering the written record and extant recordings, establishing a list of performers, cataloging recordings, and concert ephemera, creating a diachronic study of the historic building which the coffeehouse occupied, compiling biographies and discographies of performers, and understanding more about both the cultural context and sociological milieu of the club. By designing a website, www.avantgardecoffeehouse.com, and establishing a social networking presence, we will continue to aggregate information and promote community involvement in this project. These initiatives represent an expanded view of the critical foci of musicology.

Music Culture in the Omaha Tribe of North America and the Saami of Northern Scandinavia: An Analysis of the Similarities and Possible Cultural Connections between Vuolle and Be-Thae Wa-An

Trevor Wirtanen Duluth Journal of Undergraduate Research; *School of Fine Arts, University of Minnesota Duluth, Duluth, MN, 2014*

Within both the Saami of northern Scandinavian and the Native American tribe known as the Omaha, there exists a rich and complex musical culture. This essay analyzes the intricacies and aural similarities of the aforementioned cultures and strives to determine the causation of their distinct musical parallels—specifically between the be-thae wa-an of the Omaha and the vuolle of the southern Saami.

Conclusion

Much stands to be discovered within the field of ethnomusicology. The vastness of music within each nation and society, and within even each person, has each one's own draw and mysteries, universals and profundities. But it remains that music as an art, a science, a method of communication and expression, is that which hearkens longingly to the human spirit of a deeper and more glorious nature that is ours as a people is to reflect.

Questions for Discussion

1 What is "folk music?"
2 Why does it take so long for people to appreciate new music?

3 How has modern technology changed "popular music?"
4 What musical roles do we designate as either "men's" or "women's?" Where do these views come from? How are they changing, if they are?
5 Why don't we naturally understand music with different scales?
6 What is "cultural relativism?"
7 What is the difference between "popular music" and "art music?"
8 What is music? To you? To your social group? To your nation?
9 How does music influence culture? In politics? In young people's lives?
10 How do unity and variety play a part in music of most cultures?

References

Charles, D. (2017). In conversation with Gregory Young, 26 January.
Nettl, B. (1983). *The Study of Ethnomusicology*. Urbana and Chicago, IL: University of Illinois Press.
Nettl, B. (2003). *Excursions in World Music*. Upper Saddle River, NJ: Prentice-Hall.

18
PHILOSOPHY AND PSYCHOLOGY OF MUSIC

Music gives a soul to the universe, wings to the mind, flight to the imagination, life to everything.

Plato, *Laws*

When you're happy, you enjoy the music. When you're sad, you understand the lyrics.

Frank Ocean

Words make you think a thought. Music makes you feel a feeling. A song makes you feel a thought.

Yip Harburg, *PBS News Hour*

Music produces a kind of pleasure which human nature cannot live without.

Confucius

Music in the soul can be heard by the universe.

Lao Tzu

Music is a more potent instrument than any other for education, because rhythm and harmony find their way into the inward places of the soul.

Plato, *The Republic*

Summary

This chapter outlines some of the major tenets of philosophy and psychology in music and music education, and offers thoughts to inspire discussion. It differentiates between the two disciplines and the ways in which they influence performers as well as listeners, and suggests possible topics for capstone projects. Even students who are not doing projects in these sub-disciplines can benefit from reading the case studies and sample abstracts, and can delve deeper into the meaning of music and how people think about music.

Introduction

The philosophy of music is centered on how humans think about music, how it creates meaning, aesthetic experiences, emotional affect, and why it is important for everyone to have a chance to experience music. Music for its own sake is probably one of the most popular philosophical ideas from the perspective of music majors. The most important thing to remember is that there is no single correct philosophy of music. A philosophy that has been carefully and thoughtfully considered is usually appropriate for that individual. Some of the terms associated with a philosophy of music might include symbols, meaning, reflection, meditation, expressiveness, concepts, aesthetics, insight, substance, emotion, and depth. Of course there are many other ways to articulate music philosophy, and people in different cultures think about music from a variety of different perspectives (see Chapter 17, Ethnomusicology, Culture, and Popular Music).

The psychology of music has the mind as a focal point, and how it is influenced by listening to or performing music. It involves why music brings people together and connects us to each other in a way that nothing else can. Some of the questions music psychologists ask are, "When people hear or play music, how do they behave?" What happens at the level of the sound wave, the ear, and the brain when we perform or listen to music? How do musical abilities emerge and develop, and become refined as one acquires musical expertise? And what gives music its deep emotional significance and its power to influence social behavior, across vastly different cultural contexts? This subject area naturally overlaps with performance, ethnomusicology, philosophy, composition, theory, education, and interdisciplinarity (University of Oxford Faculty of Music, n.d.).

Why Students Find these Topics Intriguing

Most college students today, regardless of major, carry around with them a library of musical recordings, on their phones and/or their computers. Those who have decided on a music major and who have persisted all the way to a capstone course such as undergraduate research, undoubtedly have strong feelings about what music means to them. Often they do not take the time to reflect on or write down their deepest thoughts about the meaning of music. Every music major should be able to answer the questions "What is your philosophy of music?" or "What is your philosophy of music education?" but it takes some relatively deep thought and reflection. Projects that involve collecting and summarizing the answers to these questions provide learning experiences for both the researcher and the people being questioned. This can be done through surveys, focus groups, interviews, and/or other data collection methods.

Most music education majors have required courses in the philosophy and psychology of music education. They may not be courses focused directly on these subjects or titled as such, but it is important that somewhere in the degree program these topics are covered. It may be included in an education psychology class, or it may be covered in the methods classes. In both instrumental methods and choral methods classes, one of the first things that is talked about is the philosophy of music. The particular philosophy that one uses as a foundation for the entire degree can serve as a guide for many of the different skills a music major works on toward graduation.

Our future music teachers learn how to manage students by observing. Managing students in an instrumental music class such as a band or orchestra can be worlds apart from the same task in an English class. If a teacher has a solid grasp on philosophy and psychology of music education, and can use that effectively with students, he/she will have greater success. Conveying the deep meanings inherent in music as well as understanding how music can alter behavior are both salient topics for those who wish to teach in a way that will have lasting impact.

Psychology of Music Education

The psychology of music education centers on musical ability, the benefits of music education for the mind, and the development of musical expertise. Studies that assess private lessons are often about understanding the behavior exhibited therein and the experience that music provides for every individual. In the music education world, these are attempts to understand the way students perceive, create, respond to, and include music in their everyday life.

Several decades ago, music psychologists were concerned with testing for young students to determine whether they had the ability to study music seriously, but later conventional wisdom extolled the benefits of accepting all students, rather than selected students. The famous pedagogue, Shinichi Suzuki, espoused that every student can learn music and should be given the opportunity. An interesting study for a capstone research project might be to assess young children's ability to sing back melodic fragments before and after a year of Suzuki training. Suzuki got the idea for his landmark string teaching program from listening to young German children speak with excellent pronunciation in various dialects while he could barely pronounce the German words they were saying. They had not yet learned to read or write. He thought students at age three or four could learn violin that way, just like they learned their mother tongue. American pedagogues like Isaac Stern were so impressed at the results of this phenomenon that they traveled to Japan to see and hear it for themselves. It quickly spread around the world and millions of youth follow this method every year.

Performance anxiety is another popular topic for music majors, and almost every collegiate music school either has seminars, masterclasses, or a whole course devoted to this topic. After seeing some students incapacitated by nerves while teaching at the University of Prince Edward Island, Gregory Young developed and taught a course on the subject, using *The Inner Game of Tennis* by Timothy Gallwey as a text. The concept upon which this book is based, began on the tennis court and has spread to other performance areas, and practices throughout the world. The concept has to do with mental focus and control; a related subject area that can have profoundly beneficial effects on nervousness is mindfulness (Gallwey, 1974). There are several resources online that students can access to study the practice of mindfulness and its use in combatting nerves (see Chapter 19).

Philosophy of Music Education

There are many different philosophies of music, and every subject area will have a slightly different philosophy for the same individual. For music education, the thinking about why students should learn music, how it creates meaning and enhances quality of life, are some of the main focal points. One's philosophy is the foundation for their program. When this author (Young) was a graduate student at the University of Michigan, the dean was Paul Lehman. Part of Lehman's philosophy of music education, published later, is as follows:

> Music is one of the most powerful, most compelling, and most glorious manifestations of every cultural heritage. Music exalts the human spirit. It transforms the human experience. It's a basic instinct in every human being. That's why it holds such enormous potential to elevate and uplift the human race.
>
> (Lehman, 2002, p. 48)

Possible Topics

Philosophy

- Survey music faculty about their personal philosophies of music;
- survey music educators at all levels about their personal philosophies of music education;

- Conduct focus groups with university music majors to discuss the questions: What is music? What is art? Does a work of art have to be created by a human? Do works of art or music have to be heard or seen by a human to be art? Do they need to be intentionally created as a work of art?
- find out how mindfulness can enhance the ways we think about music;
- survey music appreciation students about music as entertainment versus music as art;
- examine the role of beauty in music;
- gather perspectives from composers about their motivations and philosophies;
- examine religion and composition in composers to see if there is a correlation with beliefs and how/why they compose;
- play differing sound files for students and inquire which ones they consider to be music/musical and why.

Psychology

- Examine how teacher feedback affects practice routines in young students;
- discover how people react to changing harmonies in a given context;
- do a meta-analysis on emotion and meaning in music in published literature;
- find out how cultural backgrounds affect perceptions of emotional content in music;
- write about music as universal language versus universal expression;
- survey international students on their perceptions of music and their backgrounds;
- document perceptions of people who choose not to listen to classical music yet enjoy it in film/theatre;
- gather data on psychological perceptions of live music;
- survey people about authentic performance practices versus movements toward electronics;
- examine how musical tastes change, standard interpretations, and how long they last;
- study visual aspects of conductors and how that affects listener's perception;
- survey people about specific subliminal messaging in music.

Sample Abstracts Submitted to NCUR

www.cur.org/conferences_and_events/student_events/ncur/archive/

A Personal Philosophy on the Importance of Music Education

Tristan Galinski, Lethbridge Undergraduate Research Journal, *4(1), 2009*

Music is a subject that is one of the most consistently threatened to be terminated at our schools. As someone who is preparing to enter into the field of education, I have decided that a clear philosophy on the importance of music would allow others to understand why I do what I do. I feel that music is one of the most important subjects a student could take and present this idea with research that validates my beliefs.

Musical Time: An Intersubjective Relationship

Michael Minkoff, Elements: Boston College Undergraduate Research Journal, *5(1), 2009*

This paper is a phenomenological exploration into the true nature of musical time. Drawing on the thought of Henri Bergson, Vladimir Jankelevitch, and contemporary philosophers of music, I propose that the nature of musical time lies within the performer and that its existence is parallel to that of the ordinary lived time of the empirical universe. We experience musical time as "mobile" (Bergson's terminology) and as a phenomenon of passing. A musician's ability to play music "in time" is governed by what I refer to as his "internal musical biological clock." However, as music is an art form that is typically performed in a group, a musician's relationship must be an intersubjective relationship where the performers' experience of time is forced by a synchronization of their internal musical biological clocks.

Living, Breathing, and Feeling the Music: How Music Is a Stronger Communicator of Emotion than Talking

Meghan Blizinski, author; Laura Ellis-Lai, mentor; Texas State Honors College Texas State University, San Marcos, 2014

This research paper examines the question "Is music a stronger communicator of emotion than verbal speaking?" This research paper is organized according to the methodology of portraiture. Portraiture is a type of writing style that allows the researcher to "paint" their findings in a artistic way rather than using a standard scientific methodology. In portraiture, the researcher uses four branches of evidence that weave together to form a flow of research; almost like using a paintbrush. The four types of evidence used are personal narratives, site/field observations, personal interviews, and database research. All of this evidence comes together to support the overarching metaphor. The metaphor for this portrait is "revisiting the past." This refers to the idea that there is no emotion in music. The listener creates the emotion they here by drawing upon experiences from the past. This portrait is split up into three different sections. The first section examines the way people associate music with a preconceived emotion. This can be completed with either positive or negative emotions. The second section touches on the idea that the type of genre and the structure of music can evoke a powerful emotional response. Finally, the third section investigates the association of a specific memory with music. As the research came to an end, it is clear that emotional response to music is greater than emotional response to verbal speaking. Therefore, it can be concluded that music is a stronger emotional communicator than verbal speaking and talking.

The "Arousal Effect": An Alternate Interpretation of the Mozart Effect

Melecio Gonzalez Jr., Glenn E. Smith IV, David W. Stockwell, and Robert S. Horton, American Journal of Undergraduate Research, *2(2), 2003*

Previous research suggests that listening to Mozart's music enhances performance on subsequent tests of spatial ability. One explanation for this result is that Mozart's music produces a positive arousal state that increases alertness and thus, enhances spatial performance. In this study, we sampled elementary students in order to investigate (1) the presence of the Mozart effect and (2) the possibility that the Mozart effect can be explained by increased levels of arousal. We assigned participants randomly to (1) listen to Mozart (Mozart group), (2) play active games (active group), or (3) sit in silence (control group) prior to completing a spatial abilities task. We expected that (1) both the Mozart and active groups would perform better on the spatial test than the control group and (2) the active group would perform better on the spatial test than the Mozart group. Pre-planned orthogonal contrasts revealed that the Mozart and active groups outperformed the control group but the Mozart and active groups performed similarly. Implications of these data for understanding the Mozart effect and for improving grade school education are discussed.

The Impact of Listening to Music on Cognitive Performance

Arielle S. Dolegui, Inquiries Journal, *5(9), 2013*

Listening to music for relaxation is common among students to counter the effects of stress or anxiety while completing difficult academic tasks. Some studies supporting this technique have shown that background music promotes cognitive performance while other studies have shown that listening to music while engaged in complex cognitive tasks can impair performance. This study focuses on the impact different genres of music, played at different volume levels, have on the cognitive abilities of college students completing academic tasks.

Conclusion

Understanding the philosophy and psychology of music is important, especially for music educators in any setting. The philosophy of music is what answers the question for every individual, of why music is important. The psychology of music describes how music makes us feel; how it connects us to each other; its interaction with human brain function; how musical ability is developed; and how it affects learning in other areas. Music enhances our understanding of some of the essential human needs: love and belonging. Music can provide a context for expression, an outlet for emotion, and a stimulus for action. It helps us to understand complexities that seem simple, and can give simple expression great depth. Music is a universal language we use to understand human emotion.

Questions for Discussion

1 Why do we reflect and think deeply about music?
2 How are psychology and philosophy related?
3 Are we hardwired to like music?
4 Does music help people focus better?
5 How does music give us an aesthetic experience?
6 How can music help us make a connection in our community?
7 What sounds are perceived as music and why?

References

Gallwey, T. (1974). *The Inner Game of Tennis: The Classic Guide to the Mental Side of Peak Performance.* New York: Random House.
Lehman, P. (2002). A personal perspective. *Music Educators Journal*, 88(5), 47–51.
University of Oxford Faculty of Music. (n.d.). Psychology of Music. Retrieved from www. music.ox.ac.uk/research/disciplines/psychology-of-music/ (accessed 2 December 2016).

19

ONLINE RESOURCES

Although online resources are constantly changing, particularly in terms of URLs and other temporary links, this chapter presents an annotated list of resources including video, audio, websites, and documents. It is divided up by user category, with some adherence to the chapter headings in this book.

Resources for All Music Majors

Peabody Institute Music Entrepreneurship and Career Center

This website has a wide range of topical areas arranged alphabetically by category for all music majors including organizations, advice, tools, and databases. www.peabody.jhu.edu/conservatory/mecc/resources.html

National Conference of Undergraduate Research (NCUR)

Since 1987 have the National Conferences on Undergraduate Research have been archiving abstracts from the thousands of students who present each year and the database is searchable. https://ncurdb.cur.org/ncur2016/archive/Search_NCUR.aspx

College Music Society (CMS)

The College Music Society promotes music teaching and learning, musical creativity and expression, research and dialogue, and diversity and interdisciplinary interaction. A consortium of college, conservatory, university, and independent musicians and scholars interested in all disciplines of music, the society provides leadership and serves as an agent of change by addressing concerns facing music in higher education. www.music.org/

College Music Symposium

College Music Symposium is the College Music Society's online journal and includes ten major service areas. From "Scholarship and Research" to "Events in Music," all are welcome to explore *College Music Symposium*'s rich heritage of scholarship and discussion and obtain information concerning the latest professional opportunities. The search feature enables the user to access *College Music Symposium*'s past work and emerging initiatives on the widest array of topics of importance to the music field. Mozart, Beethoven, Copland, and the gamelan, reviews of books and instructional materials, events in music, conference discussions—all will be found here. Through CMS forums, exploration of topics of moment to the music field are available, too. http://symposium.music.org/

TED Talks

A music search yields a variety of fascinating talks on music and medicine, music therapy, aesthetics, creativity, education, experimental music, and many other topics. These talks range in length from about 5–20 minutes and some have been viewed by over 40 million people. www.ted.com/talks/

PechaKucha 20×20

PechaKucha 20×20 is a simple presentation format where you show 20 images, each for 20 seconds. The images advance automatically and you talk along to the images. www.pechakucha.org/watch

Three Minute Thesis Competition

Three Minute Thesis Competition challenged students from across the Hamilton College curriculum to describe their thesis research and its significance to a non-specialist audience in three minutes or less. http://bit.ly/1IRdDbE

Resources for Performers

Music Performance Research

This is an open access journal: it is open for authors to submit contributions, and for readers to access without fee (see Directory of Open Access Journals, https://doaj.org). One or two issues have been published each year since 2007.

It has an international editorial board whose members are from a wide range of backgrounds and disciplines; in addition *Music Performance Research* draws on the expertise of a large pool of action editors and anonymous peer-reviewers. Its aim is to disseminate theoretical and empirical research on the performance of music. Contributions are welcome from researchers in all disciplines relevant to music performance, including archaeology, cultural studies, composition, computer science, education, ethnomusicology, history, medicine, music theory and analysis, physics, musicology, philosophy, psychology, neuroscience, and sociology. Specific topics that have been addressed to date include the role of music performance in personal development, identity, communication, and interaction; the training and health of skilled musicians; theories and models of music performance; and the foundations of musical expertise. http://mpr-online.net/

The Journal of Research in Music Performance

This is a peer-reviewed journal designed to provide presentation of a broad range of research that represents the breadth of an emerging field of study. https://ejournals.lib.vt.edu/JRMP

The AHRC Research Centre for Musical Performance as Creative Practice

Based at the University of Cambridge, the Centre created an international Performance Studies Network to enable collaborative research between scholars and performers. www.cmpcp.ac.uk/

Performance Anxiety

The following links have beneficial articles on using different techniques to benefit from performance anxiety rather than the opposite:

* http://majoringinmusic.com/reducing-music-performance-anxiety/
* www.bulletproofmusician.com/what-you-may-not-know-about-performance-anxiety/
* www.mostlywind.co.uk/performance_anxiety.html
* www.anxietycoach.com/performanceanxiety.html

Resources for Composers

The American Composers Forum

The Forum enriches lives by nurturing the creative spirit of composers and communities. It provides new opportunities for composers and their music to flourish, and engage communities in the creation, performance, and enjoyment of new music. https://composersforum.org/about

The Society of Composers Inc. (SCI)

A professional society dedicated to the promotion, performance, understanding, and dissemination of new and contemporary music. Members include composers both in and outside academia interested in addressing these concerns on a national and regional level. The governing body of the society is comprised of a national council made up of co-chairs who represent regional activities, and an executive committee made up of the editors and directors of society publications and projects. www.societyofcomposers.org/

The American Society of Composers, Authors and Publishers (ASCAP)

This is a performing rights organization which licenses and collects royalties for performance of its members' music. www.ascap.com/

Broadcast Music Incorporated (BMI)

BMI was founded in 1939 by forward-thinkers who wanted to represent songwriters in emerging genres, like jazz, blues, and country, and protect the public performances of their music. Operating on a non-profit-making basis, BMI is now the largest music rights organization in the U.S. and is still nurturing new talent and new music.

BMI is the bridge between songwriters and the businesses and organizations that want to play their music publicly. As a global leader in music rights management, BMI serves as an advocate for the value of music, representing nearly 12 million musical works created and owned by more than 750,000 songwriters, composers, and music publishers. www.bmi.com/

Interdisciplinary Resources

The Center for the Interdisciplinary Study of Music (CISM)

CISM is an association of faculty and students at the University of California, Santa Barbara (UCSB) that promotes the study of music across academic disciplines. CISM begins with the position that music is an important and powerful cultural practice, which becomes fundamental in shaping the materialities and methods of social life. By sponsoring diverse projects that engage multiple fields of knowledge, CISM works to expand the boundaries of traditional music research by creating an environment for high-level study and discussion of music that is not restricted to specialists. www.music.ucsb.edu/cism/

The Finnish Centre of Excellence in Interdisciplinary Music Research

The centre brings together people from different walks of music research. Interdisciplinary projects in music cognition, music motorics, and music and emotions aim for better understanding of both the structure and the functions of our brains in music and music in our minds. www.jyu.fi/hum/laitokset/musiikki/en/research/coe

Grieg Research School in Interdisciplinary Music Studies (GRS)

GRS aims to stimulate and develop research into music regionally, nationally, and internationally. www.uib.no/en/rs/grieg

Journal of Interdisciplinary Music Studies (JIMS)

JIMS is an international peer-reviewed journal. It aims to establish a broad interdisciplinary platform for music researchers. *JIMS* especially promotes collaborations between sciences and humanities, and provocative submissions that stimulate interdisciplinary discussion. *JIMS* is unique among international music research journals in its coverage of all epistemological approaches to all musical issues. www.musicstudies.org/

Musicology Resources

The American Musicological Society

The society's purpose is to advance scholarship in the various fields of music through research, learning, and teaching. To do this, it publishes a journal, holds an annual meeting, supports books in musicology, and offers a broad array of grants, fellowships, and awards throughout the year. www.ams-net.org/

Musicology Now

A blog sponsored by the American Musicological Society, written for the general public. It seeks to promote the results of recent research and discovery in the field of musicology (broadly construed), foster dialogue, and generate a better awareness of the subject matter. Using links, images, and sound, it references conversations within and around the academy and in the principal institutions of music making around the world. http://musicologynow.ams-net.org/2016/10/new-perspectives-on-music-therapy.html

The Department of Musicology at UCLA

The department now leads the field nationally and internationally in offering advanced training within this broader vision of the discipline. Musicologists study the history, cultural contexts, and interpretation of music. While the discipline has tended, historically, to focus largely on European art-music repertories, in recent decades it has expanded to include many other traditions as well as other regions. www.musicology.ucla.edu/

Current Musicology

Current Musicology is a leading journal for scholarly research on music. It publishes articles and book reviews in the fields of historical musicology, ethnomusicology, music theory, and philosophy of music. The journal was founded in 1965 by graduate students at Columbia University as a semiannual review. http://currentmusicology.columbia.edu/

Columbia University

The music department's mission is to support and profess scholarly and scientific inquiry into music, and equally the creative activity of music composition, at the highest levels of rigor and innovation, for both graduate and undergraduate students, specialists and non-specialists in music, and a diverse constituency that spans both across and beyond Columbia University. It contains historical musicology dissertation topics, faculty, publications, etc. http://music.columbia.edu/academic-areas/historical-musicology

The University of Southern California Thornton School of Music

The school offers a full range of academic and performance opportunities for aspiring historians, allowing students to study music in an environment where scholarship and performance interact. Musicology students will benefit from the faculty's strengths in both twentieth century and early music. The program also benefits from close links to many on-campus partners, including USC's Early Modern Studies Institute, the USC School of Cinematic Arts, and USC Annenberg School for Communication & Journalism. https://music.usc.edu/departments/musicology/

Journal of Musicology

For over 30 years, the widely-respected *Journal of Musicology*—one of few comprehensive peer-reviewed journals in the discipline—has offered articles in every period, field, and methodology of musicological scholarship. Its contributors range from senior scholars to new voices in the field. Its reach is international, with article authors and readers throughout the world. The journal publishes essential reading on long-standing problems and issues in musicology, on new ideas and approaches, and on directions in the field itself. http://jm.ucpress.edu/content/about

Empirical Musicology Review (EMR)

The journal aims to provide an international forum promoting the understanding of music in all of its facets. In particular, *EMR* aims to facilitate communication and debate between scholars engaged in systematic and observation-based music scholarship. Debate is promoted through publication of commentaries on research articles. http://emusicology.org/about

Music Theory Resources

The Society for Music Theory

The society promotes the development of and engagement with music theory as a scholarly and pedagogical discipline. It construes this discipline broadly as embracing all approaches, from conceptual to practical, and all perspectives, including those of the scholar, listener, composer, performer, teacher, and student. The society is committed to fostering diversity, inclusivity, and gender equity in the field. https://societymusictheory.org/

Websites

Teria: Music Theory Web is a very helpful site that provides exercises and learning tools for students at any level of music theory. www.teoria.com/

Reddit.com has a subforum where users can submit questions or ideas and have a community of music theorists discuss and answer questions. www.reddit.com/r/musictheory/

Duke University has a number of undergraduate articles specifically about music theory. www.dukeupress.edu/journal-of-music-theory

G Major Music Theory by Gilbert DeBenedetti is a compilation of exercises laid out in four sections: Fundamentals; Harmonic Expansions; Contextual Listening; and Harmonic Dictation. www.gmajormusictheory.org/index.html

Music Tech Teacher by Karen Garrett is a website with exercises leading toward composition. www.musictechteacher.com/index.htm

Music Theory.net provides free lessons, exercises, tools, and resources all about the various aspects of music theory. www.musictheory.net/

Music Education Resources

The Music Teachers National Association (MTNA)

The association is an organization essential not only to the professional and individual well-being of music-teaching professionals, but also a vital partner in their growth and development. It provides both a collective voice for teachers worldwide and a powerful alliance with a highly prestigious and influential group. With nearly 22,000 members in 50 states—and more than 500 local affiliates—MTNA is the pre-eminent source for music teacher support, where members embody like-minded values and commitment to their students, colleagues and society as a whole, while reaping the rewards of collaboration, continuity and connection throughout the lifetime of their careers. www.mtna.org/

National Association for Music Education (NAfME)

Among the world's largest arts education organizations, it is the only association that addresses all aspects of music education. NAfME advocates at the local, state, and national levels; provides resources for teachers, parents, and administrators; hosts professional development events; and offers a variety of opportunities for students and teachers. The association orchestrates success for millions of students nationwide and has supported music educators at all teaching levels for more than a century. www.nafme.org

Music Educators Toolbox

This set of free online resources for music teachers includes lesson plans and activities, summative and formative assessments, video examples, and documented best practices. Designed to be effective and adaptable in a wide variety of music classrooms, the resources were developed through Carnegie Hall's five-year residency in a New York City elementary/middle school. The toolbox currently features grade-specific music education resources addressing fundamentals of rhythm and meter, form and design, expressive qualities, pitch, and performing. www.carnegiehall.org/toolbox/

American Choral Directors Association

The association's aims are:

- to foster and promote choral singing, which will provide artistic, cultural, and spiritual experiences for the participants;
- to foster and promote the finest types of choral music to make these experiences possible;
- to foster and encourage rehearsal procedures conducive to attaining the highest possible level of musicianship and artistic performance;
- to foster and promote the organization and development of choral groups of all types in schools and colleges;
- to foster and promote the development of choral music in the church and synagogue;
- to foster and promote the organization and development of choral societies in cities and communities;
- to foster and promote understanding of choral music as an important medium of contemporary artistic expression;
- to foster and promote significant research in the field of choral music;
- to foster and encourage choral composition of superior quality;
- to cooperate with all organizations dedicated to the development of musical culture in America.

http://acda.org/

College Orchestra Directors Association (CODA)

CODA has provided unparalleled resources to their members and has led the charge for the promotion of academic conducting worldwide. They continue to grow their membership both nationally and internationally because of the camaraderie and friendships that CODA cultivates. https://codaweb.org/

The American School Band Directors Association (ASBDA)

The association has members all across the USA. Many states have organized their membership into active chapters and sponsor various projects for the improvement of school concert bands. States with an active ASBDA chapter benefit from a unified voice in music education, access to the best network of band directors in the United States, and wonderful relationships that last a lifetime. www.asbdaband.org/

K-12 Resources for Music Educators

This website consists of lists of different online resources for music teachers. There are sites for band teachers, vocal and choral teachers, orchestra teachers, classroom music teachers and valuable sited for all music educators. https://sites. google.com/site/k12musicresources/

Music Technology Resources

The Society for Electro-Acoustic Music in the United States (SEAMUS)

Founded in 1984, the society is a non-profit national organization of composers, performers, and teachers of electroacoustic music representing every part of the country and virtually every musical style. Electro-acoustic music is a term used to describe those musics which are dependent on electronic technology for their creation and/or performance. www.seamusonline.org

Association for Technology in Music Instruction (ATMI)

The mission of the association is to improve music teaching and learning through the integration of current and emerging technologies into the music learning environment. It does this by providing a forum for the scholarly presentation of pedagogical and technical information for music teachers in higher education. ATMI seeks to engage both specialists and non-specialists in music technology, in an atmosphere that effectively disseminates information, encourages participation, cultivates collegial relationships, and engages practice. www.atmimusic.com/

Electronic Music Midwest

The festival is dedicated to programming of a wide variety of electroacoustic music and providing the highest quality performance of electronic media. This annual festival consists of approximately nine short concerts (about one hour in length) over the course of a weekend in autumn. Their goal is to bring together vibrant and interesting artists of all forms, give them a vehicle for their expressions, and a place for them to share ideas with others. www.emmfestival.org/

Music Therapy Resources

American Music Therapy Association (AMTA)

AMTA's purpose is the progressive development of the therapeutic use of music in rehabilitation, special education, and community settings. Predecessors, unified in 1998, included the National Association for Music Therapy founded in 1950 and the American Association for Music Therapy founded in 1971. AMTA is committed to the advancement of education, training, professional standards, credentials, and research in support of the music therapy profession. www.musictherapy.org/

Musicians Without Borders

The organization uses the power of music to bridge divides, connect communities, and heal the wounds of war. Its long-term commitment allows participants the time to develop skills and talents, process grief and loss, and build bridges of reconciliation in societies divided by recent or ongoing conflict. Its professional trainers are specialized in running community music projects with people dealing with trauma, fear, and isolation as a result of war and conflict. www.musicianswithoutborders.org

Ethnomusicology Resources

The Society for Ethnomusicology

The society is a global, interdisciplinary network of individuals and institutions engaged in the study of music in all historical periods and cultural contexts. www.ethnomusicology.org/

Ethnomusicology Review

Established as *Pacific Review of Ethnomusicology* in 1984, *Ethnomusicology Review* is the graduate student publication of the UCLA Department of Ethnomusicology. It is edited by graduate students and refereed by a faculty advisory board. *Ethnomusicology Review* publishes an annual selection of scholarly articles in the current issue section of its website and posts essays, book reviews, and blogs in its Sounding Board section.

Ethnomusicology Forum

The British Forum for Ethnomusicology, in association with Routledge, publishes the scholarly journal *Ethnomusicology Forum* (formerly the *British Journal of Ethnomusicology*). Since 2011, the journal appears three times per year. Volumes focusing on a specific theme and prepared by a guest editor alternate with general issues that include a range of articles covering a broader field of interest. The journal seeks to provide a dynamic forum for the presentation of new thinking in the field of ethnomusicology. https://bfe.org.uk/ethnomusicology-forum

Music Philosophy and Psychology Resources

Philosophy of Music Education Review

The journal features philosophical research in music education for an international community of scholars, artists, and teachers. It includes articles that address philosophical or theoretical issues relevant to education, including reflections on current practice, research issues or questions, reform initiatives, philosophical writings, theories, the nature and scope of education and its goals and purposes, and cross-disciplinary dialogue relevant to the interests of music educators. www.pmer.iu.edu/

The Stanford Encyclopedia of Philosophy

The encyclopedia has a lengthy section on the philosophy of music including definitions, emotions, value, and ontology. https://plato.stanford.edu/entries/music/

Why Music Matters

The hosts of "Philosophy Talk" explore how music matters with musician and founding member of the Kronos Quartet David Harrington, in a program recorded live at Biscuits and Blues in San Francisco. https://philosophytalk.org/shows/why-music-matters

The University of Oxford: Psychology of Music

The department is concerned with understanding the psychological processes involved in listening to music, playing music, and composing and improvising music, using empirical, theoretical, and computational methods. Psychologists, computer scientists, and musicologists all make contributions to research work on music perception and cognition, computer modelling of human musical capacities, the social psychology of music, emotion and meaning in music, psychological processes in music therapy, the developmental psychology of music, music and consciousness, music and embodiment, and the neuroscience of music. www.music.ox.ac.uk/research/disciplines/psychology-of-music/

The Psychology of Music

An article by Jill Harness, University of Florida detailing how music enters our bodies and how the brain is affected by music. www.lifehack.org/articles/lifestyle/the-psychology-music.html

Certain aspects of the psychology of stage fright are covered in the links above in the performance section (performance anxiety).

INDEX